The New

ANITA DIAMANT

Jewish Wedding

A FIRESIDE BOOK
Published by Simon & Schuster
New York London Toronto Sydney Tokyo Singapore

F

FIRESIDE

1230 Avenue of the Americas
New York, New York 10020
Copyright © 1985 by Anita Diamant
All rights reserved
including the right of reproduction
in whole or in part in any form.
First Fireside Edition 1993
FIRESIDE and colophon
are trademarks of
Simon & Schuster Inc.
Designed by Edith Fowler
Manufactured in the United States of America

1   3   5   7   9   10   8   6   4   2
           10   Pbk.

Library of Congress Cataloging in Publication Data

Diamant, Anita.
The new Jewish wedding.

Includes index.
1. Marriage customs and rites, Jewish.   I. Title.
BM713.D53 1985   392'.5'088296   84-24102
ISBN 0-671-49527-5
ISBN: 0-671-62882-8 pbk.

The author gratefully acknowledges permission to reprint the following works.

"The Children of Noah: A Wedding Ceremony" by Rebecca Alpert, Linda Holtzman, and Arthur Waskow. Reprinted by permission of the authors. Copyright © 1984 by Rebecca Alpert, Linda Holtzman, and Arthur Waskow.

"The Succah and the Huppah" by Debra Cash. Reprinted by permission of the author. Copyright © 1982 by Debra Cash.

Poems from "The Song of Songs," translations by Marcia Falk. Reprinted by permission of the author. Copyright © 1973, 1977 by Marcia Falk.

"Circle Chant" by Linda Hirschhorn. Printed by permission of the author. Copyright © 1983 by Linda Hirschhorn.

"Eshet Chayil" by Susan Grossman. Reprinted by permission of the author. Copyright © 1980 by Susan Grossman.

"The Voice of God Echoes Across the Waters" by Barbara Rosman Penzner and Amy Zweiback-Levenson. Reprinted by permission of the authors. Copyright © 1984 by Barbara Rosman Penzner and Amy Zweiback-Levenson.

"The Chuppah" by Marge Piercy. Reprinted by permission of Wallace & Scheil Agency, Inc. Copyright © 1983 by Marge Piercy.

"The First Wedding in the World," "The Seven Blessings," "A Shepherd's Song in Midian," "The Mystery of Union," and "The Bride on Jubilee" by Joel Rosenberg. Reprinted by permission of the author. Copyright © 1977, 1979, 1980, 1981, 1979 by Joel Rosenberg.

The Jewish Family Book by Sharon Strassfeld and Kathy Green. Copyright © 1981 by Sharon Strassfeld and Kathy Green. Reprinted by permission of Bantam Books. All rights reserved.

"We Come Together" by Ira Wood. Reprinted by permission of the author. Copyright © 1984 by Ira Wood.

ACKNOWLEDGMENTS

I think the real reason people write books is to have the opportunity to publicly credit and thank those who made the effort not only possible but worthwhile.

Two people were crucial to the creation of this book. In addition to being my beloved and my friend, Jim Ball was also my research staff, my copy editor, my proofreader, my cheerleader, and my hand-holder. This is very much *our* book. Nor would you be reading these words were it not for Rabbi Lawrence Kushner, who, when I asked him what I should read in preparation for our wedding, wheeled around from the bookshelf behind his desk, pointed a finger at me, and said, "You should write a book about Jewish weddings." From that point on, Larry acted as official godfather to this endeavor. He was (after Jim) the first reader of every chapter. His contributions were invaluable. His influence is pervasive. He has been a great teacher.

While accumulating the facts and anecdotes that fill this book I found many wonderful teachers who were generous with their time and knowledge. They fed me lunch, challenged my assumptions, and shared their concerns and insights in addition to their expertise. Thanks are due Penina Adelman, Michele Alperin and Steven Sherriff, Rabbi Rebecca Trachtenberg Alpert, Rabbi Avram Aryan, Rabbi Al Axelrad, Nina Beth Cardin (who assisted me in consulting the files of the Jewish Women's Resource Center, National Council of Jewish Women, New York Section), Debra Cash, Pattie Chase, Howard Cooper, Lev Friedman, Rabbi Everett Gendler, Rabbi Burt Jacobson, Joshua Jacobson, Cherie Kohler-Fox, Jonathan Kremer, Riki Lippitz, Billy Mencow, Peggy McMahon, Barbara Rosman Penzner and Brian Penzner Rosman, Rosie Rosenzwieg, Reb Zalman Schachter-Shalomi, John Schechter, Drorah Setel, Rabbi Daniel Shevitz, Rabbi Jeffrey Summit, Ella Taylor, Rabbi Max Ticktin, Moshe Waldoks, and Arthur Waskow.

I owe a great debt to the artists and poets whose works grace these pages, and also thanks to the many brides and grooms whose creativity and generosity are, in fact, what this book is made of.

My thanks to Larry Moulter, my agent and friend, who helped make the *shidduch*—the match—with Arthur H. Samuelson, who was the perfect editor for this book.

The members of my *havurah*, and of my *shul*, Congregation Beth El of the Sudbury River Valley, were a source of encouragement and energy. My friends were both patient with and supportive of me this past year; thank you all, especially Laura Sperazi, Sandi Stein, and Carmen Sirianni. And I want my parents to know that their confidence in me and their *kvelling* were a constant boost.

to Jim
my beloved, my friend

CONTENTS

The main function of observance is not in imposing a discipline but in keeping us spiritually perceptive. Judaism is not interested in automatons.

Abraham Joshua Heschel,
Between God and Man

PREFACE

A LETTER FROM THE AUTHOR

Dear Readers:

It was going to be my second wedding, and I thought it would be a small affair—a few family members in the rabbi's study and then a demure little party for twenty or thirty people in the spacious home of a friend. But it was Jim's first wedding, and his guest list alone included more than thirty people. Besides, "demure" is not the kind of wedding that our rabbi, Lawrence Kushner, goes in for.

I remember that what finally sold me on the idea of having a "real" Jewish wedding was Kushner's description of *yichud*, a very ancient custom. After the ceremony the bride and groom spend ten or fifteen minutes together in a room by themselves; no receiving-line crush of well-wishers, just a little time to sit down in peace and look at each other, to share some food and relax before the party to follow. I had no idea that this simple, reasonable, and to me quite wonderful custom was part of Jewish wedding tradition. I wanted to know more.

The more I learned, the more I wanted to incorporate into our wedding ceremony and celebration. Jim and I were married under a *huppah*—a marriage canopy—in the sanctuary at Congregation Beth El in Sudbury, surrounded by one hundred loving faces. Neither of us—or any of our guests—had ever attended any wedding quite like ours. The ceremony felt both very old and entirely our own. It was simultaneously very serious and giddily joyous, sentimental but also thought-provoking. It's hard to describe. You had to be there.

The spirit of the ceremony carried over into the celebration afterward. Everyone danced and ate, and our guests entertained us with songs and jokes, cheers, poems, and magic tricks, and we all laughed until our sides ached in spite of the unseasonably hot weather. No one had a better time than Jim and me, yet in the weeks following the wedding we actually received thank-you notes from guests!

We were very fortunate to have found Larry Kushner, whose imagination and skill were the primary resources for planning our wedding, because the books that were available to help brides (not couples, mind you, just brides) plan Jewish weddings had more to say about place cards than about *yichud*. The books written by rabbis about marriage were full of what we found to be off-putting finger-wagging directions about what is and isn't "correct" according to their particular interpretations of Jewish law.

What Jim and I could have used was a book that would not only supply us with the theological and historical background we needed to understand traditional Jewish wedding practices, but would also invite our exploration of and participation in the tradition. And while we weren't interested in doing things Emily Post's way, we still needed some practical advice about such things as composing an invitation and planning a party for a hundred people. There was no such book, which is why I wrote this one.

According to Jewish law and custom, you remain a bride and groom for a full year after the wedding. I wrote *The New Jewish Wedding* as a bride during the year after our wedding, when my need for this wedding book was still very fresh. I read everything I could get my hands on that had to do with Jewish weddings; I interviewed rabbis and talked to couples who had also felt the lack of any "tools" to help plan for the kind of wedding they wanted.

During the past year, when acquaintances asked what I was doing and I told them "I'm writing a book about Jewish weddings," the most common reaction was laughter. "It's a humor book, right?" they said, immediately associating the words "Jewish wedding" with the orgy of conspicuous consumption portrayed in the film version of *Goodbye, Columbus*. That Technicolor parody has become one of the two dominant images of the Jewish wedding in our time. The other comes from *Fiddler on the Roof*, with its vague, sanitized portrayal of Orthodox/Hasidic customs that are quaint but essentially irrelevant to most American Jews. Given these models, it's no wonder that so many Jewish weddings are barely distinguishable from Protestant weddings.

I wrote *The New Jewish Wedding* to help provide alternative visions of what Jewish weddings in America today can be and of what they have in fact already become. Since the early 1970s countless couples have been married in ceremonies resembling neither *Columbus* nor *Fiddler*. This "new" approach owes a great deal to the revival of customs that were abandoned by parents and even grandparents. I am not talking about an exercise in nostalgia or an affirmation of orthodoxy but about an evolving and dynamic synthesis of modern sensibilities and Jewish tradition. These Jewish weddings, which look to the past for inspiration and meaning, reflect the concerns of our present, in which many (if not most) brides and grooms live together before marriage; in which divorce is nearly as common among Jews as among non-Jews; in which fundamental expectations about marriage have changed in response to the changing status and self-consciousness of women, both in secular culture and within the Jewish community; in which Jews fall in love with and marry non-Jews in greater numbers than ever before.

At our wedding Jim and I signed a *ketubah*, the marriage

contract that has been part of Jewish weddings since the first century. But unlike the traditional Aramaic document, with its description of the bride's trousseau and mention of only the groom's marital responsibilities, ours is an egalitarian contract that spells out in Hebrew and English our mutual commitments and obligations. I walked down the aisle side by side with Jim, who had chosen to become a Jew, and is now Yacov ben Avraham v'Sara—Jacob, son of Abraham and Sarah, the first Jews. Our *huppah* was made of Jim's beautiful, new blue-striped prayer shawl, my wedding gift to him, which was held aloft by four cherished friends—two Jews and two non-Jews, two women and two men. Rabbi Kushner chanted the ceremony both in Hebrew and in English. *Yichud*, in a dim classroom down a corridor from the commotion, was just what I'd expected: a magical relief, a moment of truth, an island of peace in a gloriously hectic day.

In Hasidism there is a willingness to ignore the boundaries between everyday life and holiness. Thus your wedding begins when you first announce your decision to marry and includes every aspect of planning and preparing for the big day. Even arguments about who gets invited and what gets served for dinner are part of the festivities. Nor is your wedding over until the last thank-you note is written, the last photograph is pasted in the scrapbook, and the last bill is paid. If you are reading this book as a bride or groom, these words are part of your wedding.

I hope you will find this book useful and challenging and that you will enjoy reading and sharing it. And I hope that your wedding is everything you want it to be.

Mazel tov!

Anita Diamant
June 12, 1984:
12 Sivan 5744

INTRODUCTION

There is no such thing as a "generic" Jewish wedding—no matter what the rabbi tells you, no matter what your mother tells you, no matter what the caterer tells you.

The rabbis who codified Jewish law, Halakhah,* made it so easy for couples to marry that the minimal requirements for carrying out a kosher Jewish wedding can be summed up in a few words: the bride accepts an object worth more than a dime from the groom, the groom recites a ritual formula of acquisition and consecration, and these two actions must be witnessed. That constitutes a Jewish wedding; the rest of the traditions associated with Jewish weddings—the canopy, the seven wedding blessings, the breaking of a glass, even the presence of a rabbi—are customs. Custom—in Hebrew, *minhag*—changes over time and differs from one nation to the next. Some Jewish wedding customs have been discarded and forgotten, and some persist with even greater symbolic and emotional power than the religious prescriptions.

Customs change to meet the needs and express the con-

* *The New Jewish Wedding* contains a number of transliterated rather than translated Hebrew and Yiddish words, because their meaning does not survive simple translation into English. Don't be intimidated even if you know neither language! Each and every non-English word is defined and explained at least once in the text, and a glossary appears at the end of the book.

cerns of people in different eras and situations. Over the centuries the Jewish wedding has been celebrated with countless variations in ritual and *minhag*. It is a dynamic and flexible tradition, and it is yours to explore and re-create.

"To be a Jew in the 20th century is to be offered a gift," wrote the poet Muriel Rukeyser. Many non-Orthodox Jews tend to believe that this gift belongs really and authentically only to traditionalists. This is simply not true. The Orthodox have no lock on Judaism, and this book documents how liberal Jews have been inspired by old practices—the *ketubah*, for example—to create new forms of non-Orthodox piety and celebration.

The New Jewish Wedding contains Halakhic standards, references to biblical, Talmudic, and mystical texts, stories, prayers, poems, and descriptions of some of the ways creative Jews have celebrated their marriages. All this is offered as a resource for people who are interested in exploring Judaism's mythic, historic, religious, gastronomic, musical, and literary "gifts" to discover what the tradition offers them today, here and now, at this threshold in their lives.

This is *not* a wedding etiquette book. Etiquette books are rather like insurance policies against doing things "wrong." They presume to instruct you in the "right" way, with the implied warning that if you do not follow the conventions properly you'll be committing terribly embarrassing mistakes. *The New Jewish Wedding* is a *minhag* book that describes the wide variety of customs and rituals that American Jews are reviving and reinventing to express themselves within a four-thousand-year-old tradition.* Furthermore, this book assumes that both partners care

---

* While I have attempted to include customs from the cultures of Sephardic (Spanish and Mediterranean) and Mizrachi (Middle Eastern) Jews, the *minhagim* in this book tend to reflect the fact that the vast majority of American Jews are descended from eastern European ancestors.

about what happens at their wedding, so it is addressed to both halves of the couple—not just to the bride.

The New Jewish Wedding is organized to help you become the architect of your own Jewish wedding. The first section, "Making the Tradition Your Own," lays the foundation for the many choices—some big and some little—you are about to make. It puts your wedding in context, which includes not only Jewish history, theology, and generations-old custom but also the concerns of modern life. Every marriage is a merger of individuals and families, and every merger creates friction. Accommodating both modern sensibilities and a four-thousand-year-old system of beliefs creates even more friction. Transforming that heat into light is the challenge of making Jewish tradition your own. And since intermarriage is one of the Jewish community's most volatile anxieties, this section also deals with the concerns of and options that are available to intermarrying couples who are looking for ways to affirm their connection with Judaism.

The second section, "Ways and Means," undertakes to help you convert your ideas and fantasies (and worries and disagreements) into a wedding. It includes descriptions of the all-important tools and props and players that go into making a Jewish wedding and the party that follows: from finding a rabbi and wording the invitation to organizing a processional and hiring a caterer.

The third section, "Celebrations and Rituals," describes the full round of parties and practices that constitute a Jewish wedding. There are customs to mark every stage of the making of a marriage—before, during, and after the "main event" under the *huppah*.

The most important difference between what you hold in your hands and a wedding etiquette book is that *The New Jewish Wedding* pays more attention to the marriage ceremony than to the wedding reception. Although Judaism places great value on celebrating, weddings are considered much more than pretexts for partying. Marriage is foremost a holy obligation—a *mitzvah*—required of every Jew. For the Jewish religious imagination the wedding has been an allegorical emblem of peak moments of sacred experience: the covenant at Sinai and the joy of Shabbat are as described in terms of the relationship between bride and groom.

The whole wedding service fills no more than a page or two. The few hundred words of the ceremony are very old, their meaning and power compressed into a dense mass, like ancient rocks striated with signs of life from a thousand generations. But custom has created a context for and given *tam*—flavor—to this almost austere ritual. Before the wedding ceremony begins,* guests are welcomed at a *kabbalat panim*—literally "receiving faces." Traditionally, this consists of two separate ceremonies: male guests go to a *chossen's tish*—groom's table—and women "attend the bride" in another room at a *hakhnassat kallah*. At some point before the *bedeken*—the "veiling" of the bride by the groom—which is attended by all the guests, the *ketubah*—marriage contract —is signed.

The wedding ceremony takes place beneath a *huppah*—a canopy supported by four poles. The liturgy is very brief. First there is an invocation, followed by *birkat erusin*—the blessings of betrothal—which include blessing and drinking from the first cup of wine. Then comes the giving and accepting of a ring, accompanied by a brief declaration of consecration called the *haray aht*. Next the *ketubah* is read aloud, the rabbi speaks to the couple, and additional prayers are offered. Then there is the chanting of *sheva b'rachot*—seven marriage blessings—which include blessing and drinking from the second cup of wine. Finally, a glass is shattered, marking the end of the ceremony. The couple then goes to *yichud*—seclusion—for ten or fifteen

* Please do not read this précis as *the* recipe for making the definitive Jewish wedding. It is only a brief description of *a* wedding, here only to familiarize you with the complement of Jewish wedding traditions that will be explained later.

minutes after the ceremony. Here they break the day-long fast that is customary for brides and grooms.

And somehow, in the heart of the ritual, custom is forgotten. Time collapses. Details like the hour, the date, the style of the bride's dress, the music—all vanish. Somehow it is the wedding of the first bride and groom, when—according to an old story—God braided Eve's hair and stood with Adam as his witness, when God pronounced the blessings and the angels shouted mazel tov. During these moments every wedding is the first and also the ultimate wedding in a four-thousand-year-old golden chain.

The last part of the book, entitled "Husbands and Wives," touches on some of the happily- and not so happily-ever-after aspects of Jewish weddings, including the traditional week of postwedding celebration and the establishment of a Jewish home.

The Talmud provides the following benediction on beholding an audience composed of Jews: "Blessed are you, Adonai our God, Sovereign of the Universe,* who discerns secrets, for the mind of each is different from the other as is the face of each different from the other." This is a blessing over diversity.[1] There have always been Judaisms. Even before the destruction of the Temple in Jerusalem in 70 C.E.,† Judaism was probably not a monolithic religion. *The New Jewish Wedding* is an expression of Jewish pluralism, and I hope it will be of use to Jews of many different backgrounds, affiliations, and beliefs—which means that I imagine everyone who reads this book will find at least one personally infuriating interpretation of Jewish law—on

---

* The words "Baruch ata Adonai Eloheynu Melech Ha-olam" introduce virtually every Jewish blessing. The most familiar English translation for the Hebrew is "Blessed art Thou, Lord our God, King of the Universe." There are many new English versions for this Hebrew formula that do not address God as a male monarch, and a number of them appear throughout this book.

† C.E., or "Common Era," is a designation that does not refer to the divinity of Jesus, as does A.D., "Anno Domini, the year of the Lord." Similarly, B.C.E. means "before the Common Era."

women, for example. While there is much that addresses (and in many cases redresses) Judaism's traditional exclusion of women from full participation in ritual life, traditional positions on issues of gender—such as women's exemption from acting as witnesses—are also included. References to the rabbi as him/her, however, do no more than acknowledge the decision to ordain women by the Reform, Reconstructionist, and Conservative movements.

Finally, there is a story told in the name of Reb Nachman of Bratslav, a seventeenth-century Hasidic master:

> A group of people who have been to a wedding are on their way home. One says, "It was a beautiful wedding. I liked the food." Another says, "It was a great wedding. The music was marvelous." Still another one says, "It was the best wedding I ever went to. I saw all my good friends there and we had a terrific time." Reb Nachman, who has overheard them, says, "Those people weren't really at a wedding."
>
> Then another wedding guest joins this group and says, "Baruch HaShem! [Blessed be the Name!] Thank God those two got together!" At that Reb Nachman says, "Now, *that* person was at a wedding!"

At the heart of this book is the wish that everyone who attends your wedding—family and friends, witnesses and guests, even bride and groom—will go home talking about the good food and the good time, *and* the fact that you two found each other and decided to invoke the blessings of family, friends, community, and tradition on your love.

PART ONE

*Making
the Tradition
Your Own*

DECISIONS, DECISIONS

When most Jews lived in small, tight-knit, intradependent communities, a wedding was a wedding: you made it as lavish and invited as many people as you could afford, but the content and meaning of the ceremony were clearly defined by Jewish tradition. The rest of it—the processional, the menu and such—were determined by local custom. No one needed a book such as this one because people understood themselves in terms of those shared customs and traditions.

For most American Jews, however, weddings are no longer a straightforward expression of shared beliefs and practices. Tradition is not a primary force in our lives. Our communities are scattered and vague. The words of the wedding ceremony lack solid moorings, and our celebrations are "mounted" by paid professionals. This state of affairs occasions a lot of wailing and breast-beating. But it has also given Jews the opportunity to rediscover and reinvent the Jewish wedding so that it can again be a mirror in which people see their own needs and dreams reflected.

Our tradition is not immediately accessible; you have to know how to "read" it. To understand the Jewish wedding you have to see it in context: how it fits into Jewish theology, the body of religious laws that govern it, the old customs and their significance for generations of brides and grooms. But an academic or even nostalgic study of antique ways is not of itself useful. Tradition dies in the library; it's got to be taken out, underlined, and disputed. Judaism needs to be held up against today's light to find out how it kindles our imaginations, because while Jewish weddings are by definition grounded in the past, their context includes the irrepressible present.

American Jews cannot marry precisely as their great-grandparents did. The world has changed too much. Marriage is not the same. Women and men may listen to each other with greater difficulty, but they do so with signs of deeper understanding. We are different kinds of Jews today, less sure of God, perhaps, but more sure of ourselves. Our weddings synthesize the sum total of Jewish experience, which includes both memory and the morning papers.

To make a wedding that is both recognizably Jewish and a personal statement requires a level of conscious decision-making that would have mystified our great-grandparents. Should we use Hebrew words in the wedding invitation? How do we walk down the aisle? What do we want to say to each other under the *huppah?* If we do *yichud,* how can we have a receiving line? How are we going to make this wedding Jewish? How Jewish are we going to make this wedding?

The more numerous the choices, the greater the likelihood of disagreements and conflict between brides and grooms, among families, between tradition and personal style. There's a Yiddish saying, "No *ketubah* was ever signed without an argument." The result of all this learning, choosing, and even arguing is more than just a party. As rites of passage, weddings clarify and express a great deal about the people under the *huppah.* A wedding is a public announcement and demonstration of who you are as a couple. When you draw on Jewish tradition—borrowing, revising, even rejecting, in essence struggling to create meaning with it—the tradition becomes yours.

THE TRADITION OF MARRIAGE

The first of the 613 *mitzvot* (commandments) in the Torah is "Pe'ru ur-vu" ("Be fruitful and multiply"). Judaism sanctifies every dimension of human experience—from birth to death, from eating to eliminating. Sexuality and procreation are sanctified by marriage, the primary purpose of which is the creation of new life. Every wedding sets the stage for the next generation of "the children of Israel." The Talmud records that "one who does not participate in 'be fruitful and multiply' causes God's presence to vanish."[1] Indeed, marriage is seen as the prototypical act of creation. The Zohar, the great book of Jewish mysticism, states: "God creates new worlds constantly. In what way? By causing marriages to take place."[2]

In the Midrash, the imaginative rabbinic literature "somewhere between commentary and fantasy . . . that sprouts up in the spaces between the consecrated words of Scripture,"[3] the creation of male and female inspired a fabulous tale about the first wedding.

> The wedding of the first couple was celebrated with pomp never repeated in the whole course of history. God Himself, before presenting Eve to Adam, attired and adorned her as a bride. . . . The angels surrounded the marriage canopy, and God pronounced the blessings upon the bridal couple, as the *hazzan* does under the *huppah*. The angels then danced and played musical instruments for Adam and Eve in the ten bridal chambers of gold, pearls and precious stones that God had prepared for them.[4]

The ongoing work of making marriages is considered so vital that heaven is imagined as constantly astir with news of them. According to the Talmud, "Forty days before the formation of a child, a Voice proclaims in heaven: 'So-and-so's daughter is to marry so-and-so's son.' "[5]

The Midrash portrays God as a perpetual *shadchan*, or matchmaker, for the whole world:

> Once a Roman matron asked Rabbi Jose bar Halafta: "How long did it take the Holy One, blessed be He, to create the world?"
>
> He said to her, "Six days."
>
> "From then until now what has He been doing?"
>
> "The Holy One, blessed be He, is occupied in making marriages."
>
> "And is that His occupation?" the woman asked. "Even I can do that. I have many men slaves and women slaves and in one short hour I can marry them off."
>
> "Though it may appear easy in your eyes," he said, "yet every marriage is as difficult for the Holy One, blessed be He, as the dividing of the Sea of Reeds." Then Rabbi Jose left her and went on his way.
>
> What did the matron do? She took a thousand men slaves and a thousand women slaves, placed them in two rows and said, "This one should wed that one, and this one should wed that one." In one night she married them all. The next day they came before her —one with a wounded head, one with a bruised eye, another with a fractured arm, and one with a broken foot.
>
> "What is the matter with you?" she asked.
>
> Each one said, "I do not want the one you gave me."
>
> Immediately the woman sent for Rabbi Jose bar Halafta and said to him: "Rabbi, your Torah is true, beautiful, and praiseworthy."
>
> "Indeed a suitable match may seem easy to make, yet God considers it as difficult a task as dividing the Sea of Reeds," Rabbi Jose acknowledged.[6]

Nor does God disappear once a match is made. According to the *Midrash*, after Eve's creation, Adam was called *esh*—fire. Eve was also called *esh*, but when they married, two of the letters of God's name *(Yud-Hay-Vav-Hay)* were added to each of theirs. Adam's name became *aleph-Yud-*

shin, ish—man—and Eve's name became *aleph-shin-Hay, ishah*—woman. Thus when God's presence is absent from a marriage, there is only *esh* and *esh*, "fire consuming fire."[7]

Although the rabbis considered marriage divine in origin and a holy obligation, they also understood that as a human enterprise it was subject to great difficulties and even failure. Keeping God's name in a marriage is no easy task, so the Talmud devotes great attention to the rights and responsibilities of brides and grooms, wives and husbands. The laws regarding marriage cover everything from dowries to sexual conduct to divorce; they are complex, rigorous, often contradictory, and, like all of Halakhah (Jewish law), undeniably patriarchal.

The commandment to marry is directed toward men. According to the Talmud, a wife can save a young man from "sinful thoughts,"[8] and "Any man who has no wife is not a man [a complete human being]."[9] Marriage to a good woman is often described as the source of happiness and blessing for a man. (The Talmud seems generally less concerned with women's happiness.)

Still, Halakhah was undisputably progressive for its time in establishing certain rights for women: minor girls may not be betrothed, and women have the legal right to refuse any suitor, no matter what their parents command. Although only men can grant divorces, women are entitled to sue for divorce on some grounds, including sexual incompatibility. Conjugal rape, a legal conundrum in our time, is explicitly prohibited in the Talmud. And despite the fact that wives are "acquired" in much the same manner as property, men are required to treat them with respect and tenderness or risk God's wrath.

While Jewish law regulated marriage, Jewish weddings inspired the dreams, prayers, and creative energies of hundreds of generations. "Be fruitful and multiply" is not only God's wish, it is the articulate cry of a people with a precarious place in the world. Among survivors of the Holocaust there is a saying "To dance at a Jewish wedding is to dance on Hitler's grave." For every generation weddings are a glimpse into the future, a repudiation of past griefs, and a celebration of the here and now.

In *Yiddishkeit's* (Judaism's) pantheon of colorful characters the *shadchan* is one of the stars. During the Middle Ages matchmakers were learned men and rabbis, but by the eighteenth century the profession had changed, and they tended to be fast-talking used-car-salesman types who glossed over physical defects and large discrepancies in age with theatrical flourishes of rhetoric. Even so, because his work was considered so important, the matchmaker remained a beloved rogue; according to the Yiddish proverb, "God does not punish the *shadchan* for telling lies." The profession finally withered away in Europe during the Enlightenment, when the idea of romantic love as a legitimate basis for marriage swept the *shtetl*, inspiring dread among traditionalists, who foretold the demise of the family-arranged marriage and predicted the imminent death of Judaism itself.

MODERN OPTIONS

For most Jews today marriage is no longer so much a commandment as it is an option. While Judaism places an absolute value on marriage, Jews are part of a secular culture in which marriage is no longer necessary to fulfill a man's or a woman's financial, social, or sexual needs. In America today the dividing line between adults and children is not marriage and the establishment of a family so much as it is work and the launching of a career. Then, too, marriage has acquired a rather dismal reputation in our time. Even Jewish marriages, which once seemed immune to the divorce epidemic, now have at best a one-in-three chance of lasting for a lifetime.

American Jews tend to marry and have children later than their parents did. Even remaining single is no longer the shame it once was. (Indeed, the now significant number of unmarried adults in the Jewish community is a recent and unprecedented development.) Still, an overwhelming majority of Jews do exercise their option—and perform the *mitzvah*—by marrying.

Some see the intersection of Jewish tradition and modern life as a pitched battle, but others have found that there are valuable opportunities for creative thought and practice even in the thorniest conflict between Halakhah and modern sensibility. Jewish weddings are often a watershed in this meeting of old and new, offering many people their first opportunity to make Jewish decisions as adults.

For example, the most pervasive challenge to tradition in recent years has been the transformation of women's self-consciousness and social roles both in secular culture and within the Jewish community. In planning a wedding, women and men who are committed to an egalitarian marriage sometimes find themselves confronted with a dichotomy in Jewish thought. While the tradition often eulogizes the strength and wisdom of women, it also features a deep-seated distrust of them. And though the Talmud stresses respect for women, it also dictates a distinctly separate role for them. The "inferiority" or "equivalence" of that role is currently a subject of discussion and debate in all corners of the Jewish community.[10]

The traditional Jewish model of marriage echoes with ancient ways of being and doing, so for men and women who want to live and love in ways the patriarchs never imagined, weddings can be a source of some ambivalence. But weddings can also resolve that ambivalence in ways that both affirm traditional Jewish respect for women and express personal commitments to equality.

In many Jewish weddings today the active participation of women has replaced what was once a ceremony of their ritual acquisition. *Ketubot* are written to spell out reciprocal responsibilities, and the wedding liturgy is amended to literally give women a voice under the *huppah*. Jewish women marry under canopies that are made of their own prayer shawls; female rabbis and scholars officiate at weddings; women sign *ketubot* as witnesses and chant the seven wedding blessings for their sons and daughters. Even in more traditional communities where some of these practices are considered too radical, women are vocal, visible participants in weddings, in which only a few years ago they were permitted no active role.

The Jewish mystics saw each wedding as the beginning of a whole new world. An egalitarian wedding ceremony can announce that the couple under the *huppah* have reflected on the nature of their vows and the shape of the life they plan to build together. "Marriage between equals" may sound like a cliché; in fact it is a challenge to create a new world.

HOW JEWISH A WEDDING DO YOU WANT?

But the primary choice facing two Jews planning a wedding today is whether to make the event recognizably Jewish at all. "Do we go to a justice of the peace and forget about religion and tradition altogether?" If the answer to that question is no, you are confronted with choices about how to make it a Jewish wedding, which for most people means finding resources—such as this book. In general, the most important resource is the rabbi, who not only officiates but guides and advises couples about the Jewish content of their weddings. Thus it becomes important to make a good *shidduch*—a good match—with a rabbi. "Rabbi" means "teacher." The best matches are those that encourage exploration, discussion, and enough self-confidence so you can make some Jewish decisions for yourselves.*

Jewish decision-making about a wedding is part of the process of establishing a Jewish home, a process that can become a source of conflict. When a Jew from a nonobservant family marries someone from a religiously observant Jewish home, the term "intermarriage"—with all its emotional connotations—is not altogether inappropriate. Differences in belief, identity, and practice may become sore points, even between two Jews who belong to the same synagogue. Despite great and well-known variations in practice, many people are still apt to say such things as *"This* is the way Jews have always done things at weddings, so this is the way we have to do it."

Most of us identify the traditional with the terms we learned from our parents, and families do far more picking and choosing among Jewish customs and practices than they realize. In fact, people tend to value and perpetuate those elements of their tradition that most closely coincide with their own life-styles.[11] Understanding that every family's way of doing things is only one expression of the varied and dynamic civilization that is Judaism creates room for compromise. A respect for Jewish pluralism means that your wedding can become a synthesis of rather than a battle between differing views.

ANTICIPATING CONFLICT

But even with the most supportive rabbi and lots of mutual respect and all kinds of Jewish self-confidence, weddings are stressful events. Planning a wedding puts an

---

* See the section "Choosing a Rabbi" for a full discussion of how to find and work with a compatible teacher.

understandable strain on everyone's nerves, but a heated argument about who will be marching down the aisle is rarely just the result of working under a deadline. When you and your mother—or you and your beloved—start yelling at each other about the processional, it's safe to assume that you're not really arguing about who's on first.

Weddings are emotionally charged turning points, not only in the lives of the bride and groom but also and especially for their families. A wedding is a rite of passage that signals major life changes and raises issues about intergenerational dependence and independence. But there is often more involved than issues of the losing-a-son, gaining-a-daughter variety. Life-cycle events are embedded in everything else going on in the family.[12] Your wedding may precipitate conflicts about things that don't seem to have very much to do with the event at hand—extended family relationships and even your parents' own marriage.

Such interfamily dynamics get played out during another conflict-prone process—the merger of two families that have different histories, customs, and expectations about what a wedding should be. Although many families do their best to minimize tensions with soon-to-be relatives, even minor misunderstandings deserve careful handling. In such an emotion-charged setting, little things tend to get blown out of proportion and can sour relationships for years to come. The more resolution and harmony you can achieve in the months prior to a wedding, the happier the day will be. If things get really out of hand, in some cases a meeting with the rabbi or even a family counselor may help clarify issues.

Establishing who pays for what is one of the most common causes of inter- and intrafamily conflict. In the past, things were a little more clear-cut. In many communities the groom's family assumed all wedding costs; after all, the bride's family was providing the dowry. More recently it's become customary for the bride's parents to assume the entire cost (a kind of latter-day dowry), except for such things as the groom's clothes and other incidentals, which became his family's responsibility. But today, sometimes even last generation's customs don't address current needs.

Couples who have been financially independent for many years often prefer—and sometimes are even better equipped—to pay their own wedding bills. In such cases, parental gifts of money become a way of "dowering" the marriage. It is increasingly common for wedding costs to be shared among two or three parties: the groom's family, the bride's family, and the couple. This may sound fair and equitable in theory, but in practice it's a complicated way to go.

Money is a potent symbol. For many people, giving money is an important way of expressing love. A parent's refusal to pick up the tab for his child's wedding celebration is a powerful statement of disapproval. Likewise, refusing a parent's offer to pay can represent rejection. Money also determines control. It's rare (but not unheard of) for parents to foot the bills without expecting to influence decision-making in proportion to their contribution. They who write the checks generally, and reasonably, want a hand in the product.

A simple, straightforward way to help minimize some of the more task-oriented family conflicts (which are often the staging ground for issues of control) is for the bride and groom to prepare a few lists before sitting down with the parents. First, draw up a list of "nonnegotiable" items—aspects of the wedding over which you are not prepared to compromise. These will obviously vary from couple to couple and can range from refusal to have anything to do with rented clothing to the content of the ketubah. The second list includes things about which you don't feel quite as strongly and concerning which you are willing to compromise—for instance, the wording of your invitation, music for the processional, the menu. Since these negotiations entail give-and-take, this list might include tasks you have every intention of letting your mother "win": floral arrangements, a family dinner before the wedding, accommodations for out-of-town guests, and so forth.

WHEN JEWS MARRY NON-JEWS

Family conflict rarely reaches a greater emotional pitch than when a Jewish child announces a decision to marry a non-Jew. Intermarriage is seen as a complete break with tradition and a threat to the continuation of the Jewish people. Many couples are bewildered and angered by this viewpoint, which is more or less the "party line" of the entire Jewish community.[13]

Very few rabbis will officiate at a marriage between a Jew and a non-Jew. Orthodox and Conservative rabbis simply will not participate, nor will most Reform or Reconstructionist rabbis. (A 1978 survey of Reform rabbis showed that only 157 of 1268 said they had officiated at an intermarriage.)[14] Couples who feel personally rejected by this position rarely understand its basis in Jewish law.

A Jewish wedding has legal standing when two witnesses see the bride accept a ring from the groom and hear him say, "Haray aht m'kudeshet li b'taba'at zu k'dat Moshe v'Yisrael." ("With this ring you are consecrated to me [as my wife] according to the laws of Moses and Israel.") The rabbi doesn't marry the bride and groom; they marry each other. The *haray aht* constitutes a formal contract. Thus if one of the parties is not bound "by the laws of Moses and Israel," the contract is not binding; it is void.

Another reason for the reluctance of rabbis to participate in intermarriages is that the major function of Jewish weddings is the consecration of Jewish homes and the establishment of Jewish families. Despite assurances and good intentions, recent experience with intermarried couples in-

dicates that very few children of intermarriages ever identify as Jews.

Simply put, the American Jewish community perceives
intermarriage as a threat and is frightened. The fact that
predictions about the imminent demise of the Jewish people date from ancient times does not allay these fears, in
part because the openness of American society poses an
unprecedented challenge to the maintenance of a distinct
Jewish identity.

Still, community hysteria about intermarriage over-
whelms and ignores the dilemmas that face many Jews in
love with non-Jews. The prospect of marrying a non-Jew
sometimes raises issues of Jewish identity. Suddenly it occurs to you that you want your children brought up as
Jews. You realize that you would feel bereft if your wedding didn't take place under a *huppah*. Perhaps for the first
time you are wrestling with what it means to be a Jew.

It is difficult and certainly less enjoyable to plan a wedding while struggling with parental pressure, community
disapproval, and personal issues of identity and affiliation.
However, in most cities and towns there are individuals—
among them counselors at Jewish agencies and some rabbis
—who are willing to listen to you and discuss your options
for affirming a connection with Judaism; some of these follow.

Conversion. Non-Jews planning to marry Jews may be
facing dilemmas of their own: What is my religious/ethnic
identification? What does it mean for me to be marrying a
Jew? If it means so much to her/him to raise our children
as Jews, and I agree to help, what part can I play? What is
a Jewish home and how do I fit into one?

Some non-Jews—especially those who have lived with
their Jewish partners before deciding to marry—find that
their lifelong curiosity about Judaism and association with
Jews has now led to a more formal commitment. And while
conversion for the sake of marriage has always been dis-

couraged by Jewish law, marriage has undeniably prompted a great many sincere conversions that have enriched the Jewish people.

Conversion to Judaism is largely a matter of study, which is usually directed by a rabbi. The amount of time required to prepare for conversion can vary from six months to two years or more, depending on the rabbi's requirements and the student's diligence. In addition to study, Jewish law requires *mikvah* (ritual immersion) for men and women, and circumcision or ritual circumcision (drawing one drop of blood from an already circumcised foreskin) for men. Converts also meet with a *bet din*—a rabbinical court—which usually consists of three rabbis, who examine the "candidate" about his or her knowledge of Judaism. (People are almost never "failed," since rabbis will not propose unqualified candidates.) Sometimes Jews by choice are also offered the opportunity to publicly acknowledge their conversion during Shabbat services.

Once a non-Jew has become a Jew, intermarriage is no longer an issue. Indeed, Jewish law prohibits Jews by choice from being referred to as "converts." As Jews, they are altogether welcome under the *huppah*; the dilemma is resolved.*

*A Jewish-Style Wedding.† "Kosher-style" food is not really kosher food, because, despite its identification with Jewish

---

* For a more nearly complete discussion of conversion, see the chapters on intermarriage and conversion in *The Third Jewish Catalog*, compiled and edited by Sharon Strassfeld and Michael Strassfeld (Philadelphia: Jewish Publication Society of America, 1980).

† Conversion is the only response to intermarriage that satisfies the entire Jewish community, and, even so, Orthodox Jews recognize only conversions supervised by Orthodox rabbis. The state of Israel currently shares this position.

The following "options" are of an entirely different order. The weddings described below can be very beautiful and meaningful and provide a connection with Judaism. They are, however, extremely controversial in the Jewish community. These ceremonies do not seek to conform to Jewish law, which is clear and inflexible on the subject of intermarriage.

culture (bagels and knishes), the laws of *kashrut** are not necessarily followed. Similarly, a wedding between a Jew and a non-Jew—even one that is held in a synagogue and conducted by a rabbi—cannot really be a Jewish wedding because the laws of *kiddushin* that govern marriage have not been observed.

"Jewish-style" ceremonies are mostly used when the Jewish partner identifies as a Jew and the non-Jew has no religious affiliation and is perhaps willing to make some commitment to help establish a Jewish home. While this kind of wedding has no standing in Jewish law, for some couples it can be a way of affirming their connection to Judaism. In general, the entire "normative" Jewish liturgy is not used in "Jewish-style" weddings; for example, the *haray aht* may be omitted or changed. But other Jewish sources (Song of Songs, Psalms, Proverbs, and secular Jewish love poetry) can create a wedding that is clearly infused with Jewish *tam*—flavor.

The small minority of rabbis who officiate at weddings between Jews and non-Jews generally deal with interfaith couples on a case-by-case basis. They perform intermarriages selectively, hoping to increase the likelihood that the non-Jewish spouse will eventually convert and/or that children will be raised as Jews. These rabbis often have clear limits about the circumstances under which they will perform weddings. For example, most will not co-officiate with a member of the clergy of another faith, and most require a few meetings with the couple. Some rabbis will officiate at an intermarriage only if both the bride and groom will sign a marriage contract that affirms a commitment to Jewish continuity.

There are very few published resources for couples interested in this kind of ceremony. One notable exception is *The Children of Noah* by Rabbi Rebecca Alpert, Rabbi Linda Holtzman, and Arthur Waskow, a ceremony "intended for

---

* The system of laws that govern what and how Jews eat.

use in a Jewish context to affirm and make holy the marriage of two people who are 'children of Noah'—one of whom is a Jew." *The Children of Noah* ceremony* echoes the Jewish wedding ritual: the bride and groom stand within a circle, drink from glasses of water, and marry each other with words inspired by the Book of Hosea. Its major motif is the "rainbow covenant," God's promise after the flood not to threaten life on earth again if the entire human race abides by seven commandments.

Civil Ceremonies. Many rabbis who are sympathetic to the dilemmas of intermarrying couples suggest that intermarriages be performed by a secular authority on neutral territory, because they feel that a rabbi's participation or even presence may suggest community sanction of the wedding. In a non-Jewish setting, in a ceremony performed by a judge or justice of the peace, the use of Jewish symbols and content is clearly but solely the personal expression of the couple.

A civil ceremony is a good option for couples in which the non-Jewish partner is still committed to his or her faith background and wants to include, for example, a reading from the New Testament. People seeking an altogether "universalist" or "ecumenical" wedding may do best by writing a ceremony that expresses the beliefs they value and share in both of their traditions.

Mercenaries. A Jew and a non-Jew can purchase a Jewish wedding complete with all the trimmings. "Mercenary" rabbis (so called by their disapproving colleagues) make comfortable livings selling their services to families who insist on a Jewish wedding for couples who don't much care one way or the other. These rabbis don't usually require meetings with the bride and groom prior to the wedding but ask for a hefty fee—often payable in advance.

* See Appendix for the entire ceremony.

PART TWO

*Ways
and Means*

PLANNING
THE WEDDING

CHOOSING A RABBI

The person who reads the wedding blessings at a Jewish wedding is called the *mesader kiddushin*, the one who "orders" the ceremony of *kiddushin*, or sanctification. That person does not "marry" the bride and groom; they marry each other. According to Halakhah, a *mesader kiddushin* must be a Jew who is knowledgeable about Jewish laws regarding weddings and marriage. It is not strictly necessary for a rabbi to officiate at a wedding for the event to be kosher and binding.

Not only do cantors commonly officiate at weddings but other nonordained Jewish scholars, educators, and community leaders also are available to do the honors, many of whom are state-licensed to perform Jewish weddings. Some couples prefer the intimacy of a ceremony led by a close friend or relative who may not be licensed; the civil documents may be taken care of by a judge or justice of the peace.

However, few people are Jewishly self-sufficient or self-confident enough to attempt a rabbiless wedding. Besides, the weight of custom is very strong in this regard, dating back to Maimonides, the great rabbinic authority of the twelfth century, who advised the Jews of Egypt that marriages required the supervision of an ordained rabbi.[1] And today rabbis represent more than Jewish law and learning at weddings.

A wedding may be Jewishly legitimate in all ways but not be recognized by the state, and generally civil weddings have no Jewish status. As an official of both the Jewish community and also as an agent of the secular authorities, a rabbi ensures by his participation that the marriage will be recognized as legal by all interested parties—not the least of whom are the families of the bride and groom.

Often there is no question of "choosing" a rabbi. If either or both of you belong to a synagogue, the congregation's rabbi will expect to officiate, and if you are planning a "home town" wedding, your parents' congregational rabbi —who may or may not be the rabbi of your childhood— will probably conduct the ceremony. If your best friend happens to be a rabbi and you belong to a congregation *and* there's a family rabbi in the picture, the ceremony can be divided among them in any number of ways. Many rabbis have some experience "sharing" a wedding with colleagues; this can be done easily and gracefully, without giving offense to anyone.

But given the substantial number of Jews who are unaffiliated with any religious institution, couples often find that they have little or no idea of where to begin looking for a rabbi. Childhood images of The Rabbi persist far into adulthood, which means that some people are intimidated by, suspicious of, and sometimes even hostile to anyone who bears the title. It's useful to think about selecting a rabbi the same way you go about choosing any other professional whose services you wish to use. If you wouldn't pick a dentist at random, don't try that approach with a rabbi. Ask people whose opinion you trust and/or people who are familiar with a particular rabbi; go to see rabbis "in action," officiating at a ritual or leading a worship service. And expect to talk to two or three rabbis before making a decision.

If you want to speak to Reform rabbis, '
the Union of American Hebrew Congre₂
the names of congregations in or near you.
For information about Conservative rabbis,
Synagogue of America office may be of help. ᴄ
people who are interested in having their marriage ₃
nized by an Orthodox rabbi will already be familiar w.
the local rabbis and *shuls* (synagogues), but if you're new in
town, a visit to the kosher meat market may be all you need
by way of a referral service.

If you are in any way affiliated with a university, the
campus Hillel rabbi is a logical candidate, since you are
already part of his or her "congregation." But unaffiliated
Jews often call upon Hillel rabbis with the expectation that
people who work with college students are more flexible,
liberal, or easier to approach. There are all kinds of Hillel
rabbis, from Classical Reform to Hasidic. Some campus
rabbis are more accessible than some congregational rabbis,
but it's unwise to make too many assumptions about any
rabbi's style or theology based on age, gender, formal affiliation, or congregation. The lines between Reform and
Conservative Judaism have been smudged for a long time
now, and there are many orthodoxies. Reconstructionism
and the *havurah* movement have added new voices to the
American Jewish chorus.*

As a last resort, the white pages of the telephone book in
most cities and towns will include some listing under the
word "Jewish." A community center or Jewish counseling
service is worth a try, if not for direct referrals, then for
the names of other organizations that can be of help. Cities
with sizable Jewish communities often publish a Jewish
directory that can be obtained through any number of organizations, from B'nai Brith to the United Jewish Appeal
office.

* If you have trouble locating information about either of these latter
Judaisms in your community, call the Reconstructionist Rabbinical Col-
lege in Philadelphia or the National Havurah Committee office in New
York City.

Once you have a list of likely candidates, attend a service or lecture, and if you like what you see, approach the rabbi afterward and explain why you're there and that you'd like to make an appointment to discuss your wedding plans. (This is an excellent method of capturing the attention of even the busiest rabbi.)

A few practical considerations can be dispatched over the phone—first of all, there's the question of the wedding date. If you care about your ceremony, find a compatible rabbi before reserving a hall or hiring a caterer. Both the bride and the groom—and only the bride and groom—should attend meetings with the rabbi. (Mothers are *not* invited, no matter how involved they are in planning the wedding.)

At the initial interview you can expect to be asked about yourselves in some detail and to be questioned about family history and religious background, education, career, previous marriages, children, and individual and common hopes for your marriage. Few rabbis will be surprised if you mention that you are living together. Indeed, you may well be asked to explain why you have decided to marry. (Even very traditional rabbis will not turn you away on grounds of previous "immorality." While premarital sex and cohabitation are forbidden by Jewish law, neither renders you unfit for marriage.) If either of you has been married before, Orthodox and Conservative rabbis will ask if a *get*—a Jewish writ of divorce—has been obtained.*

Before meeting with the rabbi ask yourselves what you want from a rite of passage. What is your preferred style of celebration? How, for instance, do you mark birthdays? With elegant, candle-lit dinners or with paper hats and noisemakers or with both? Think about weddings you've been to, weddings you've read about, weddings you've seen in the movies. What did you like about them and what made you uncomfortable?

* See the section "Divorce."

And have some specific questions ready for your first meeting. You might ask him/her to describe the most beautiful wedding he/she ever conducted—what made it special? Although the wedding liturgy is simple and brief, rabbis develop a pattern or sequence they find meaningful and effective. Ask him/her to describe what he/she usually does. If you are concerned about non-Hebrew-speaking guests (both Jewish and non-Jewish), ask how much of the ceremony will be translated into English. If you are sensitive to language that refers to God only in the masculine gender, you should say so, and perhaps ask how he/she translates the phrase "Baruch ata Adonai"—a phrase that is repeated many times during the wedding. Try to determine the rabbi's willingness to incorporate your ideas for personalizing the service; bring up any ideas you may have about poems, songs, or individuals you would like included.

Most rabbis want to get to know the people for whom they act as *mesader kiddushin* and will expect to meet with you a number of times. Two to five meetings are standard, and content varies greatly. Some premarital meetings may take the form of counseling about aspects of your relationship—from sexuality, to the way you argue, to how you manage money. Others may consist of instruction by the rabbi about the meaning of marriage in Jewish tradition. You may be asked to read and study in preparation for your meetings together.

The rabbi will probably want to spend as much time talking about marriage as about your wedding plans. Since a wedding marks the establishment of a new Jewish home, the rabbi may want to discuss some of the following topics: observance of Shabbat and the yearly cycle of holidays, the placing of a mezuzah at the door, keeping a kosher kitchen, raising Jewish children, and affiliating with Jewish organizations.

Some people think of the rabbi as a kind of spiritual chauffeur—someone who simply takes you where you tell him/her to go. Rabbis are understandably put off by couples who approach them with lists of "demands." While it's important to communicate self-confidence in your own abilities to make Jewish decisions and to be clear about your basic requirements, there are limits to the process of give-and-take.

The rabbi has obligations beyond providing you with help and understanding. He/she also has a responsibility to Jewish tradition, as he/she understands and interprets it. There are some things every rabbi feels he/she cannot do or condone and still remain true to his/her understanding of Halakhah, of the *mitzvot*, of the Torah. These vary greatly from one rabbi to the next, but it would be disrespectful, pointless, and self-defeating to insist on something your rabbi cannot in conscience go along with.

One of the most difficult subjects for many couples—and not a few rabbis—is payment. Generally, if you are a member of a congregation, the rabbi's services are covered by dues or membership fees. (Even then, a gift of *tsedakah* —charity—given in the rabbi's name is appropriate and thoughtful.) If you are not members, the rabbi will inform you of his/her fee. If the amount he/she mentions would cause a hardship, most rabbis will do their best to accommodate you. If the wedding will be held out of town, the rabbi should, of course, be reimbursed for expenses.

Some people are outraged that rabbis charge anything at all to preside at weddings. Others think of payment to the rabbi as a sort of tip. Rabbis are professionals whose services are worth compensation. The time they spend meeting with couples and officiating at weddings is time away from family and other responsibilities. Ask when and how payment should be made; the rabbi should never have to send you a bill.

It is customary to invite the rabbi and his/her spouse to the party following your wedding. (The same holds true for cantors and their spouses.) The rabbi and/or cantor should receive an invitation as a courtesy. Be sensitive to his/her observance of the dietary laws. If he/she keeps kosher, platters of shrimp would be an embarrassment for all. In the past the rabbi's presence at a wedding celebration proved the importance of the family. Do not be disappointed, however, if your rabbi declines your invitation or stays at the festivities for only a short time. It's difficult to enjoy a party at which you are acquainted only with the bride and groom, especially since rabbis report that wedding guests often feel compelled to be on their best behavior around any member of the clergy. This could even put a damper on the merriment, which would run contrary to the *mitzvah* of rejoicing the bride and groom.

WHEN AND WHERE

> Jewish ritual may be characterized as the art of significant forms in time, as *architecture of time.* Most of its observances—the Sabbath, the New Moon, the festivals, the Sabbatical and the Jubilee year—depend on a certain hour of the day or season of the year. It is, for example, the evening, morning, or afternoon that brings with it the call to prayer. The main themes of faith lie in the realm of time. We remember the day of the exodus from Egypt, the day when Israel stood at Sinai; and our Messianic hope is the expectation of a day, of the end of days.
>
> Abraham Joshua Heschel,
> *The Sabbath*[2]

You can raise a *huppah* anywhere. Although there are customs and conventions about "appropriate" locations for weddings, just about any place can be made a holy place by human action and intention. Time, however, is another matter. Fully one out of seven days—Shabbat—is forbidden, and there is a list of dates on the Jewish calendar when weddings are proscribed.* Thus weddings are integrated into a yearly cycle during which "Every hour is unique and the only one given at the moment, exclusive and endlessly precious."[3]

Weddings are forbidden on the Sabbath not only because of the inevitable work and travel that would violate the laws prescribing rest from all labor but also because of the injunction that every simcha—every joy—be celebrated and savored individually. According to Jewish law, "One should not mix rejoicing with rejoicing." The combining of two joys risks that one or both of them will not be given its due, which is why double weddings are discouraged.

Weddings may not be held on the major holidays and festivals, including Rosh Hashanah, Yom Kippur, Passover, Shavuot, and Sukkot. (Hanukkah and Purim are exempt from this prohibition.) In Orthodox and Conservative practice there are two extended periods of public mourning during which marriages are not solemnized: the three weeks between the seventeenth of Tammuz and the ninth of Av, which generally fall in July and/or August and commemorate the destruction of the Temple, and the Omer period, between Passover and Shavuot, seven weeks that usually fall in April and May. Lag b'Omer, the thirty-third day in the counting of the Omer, is exempt from this prohibition and is a very popular day for weddings in Israel. In all cases ask your rabbi and consider your family's level of observance before deciding on a summer date. Likewise, the fast days of Tisha b'Av, the tenth of Tevet, the seventeenth of Tammuz, and the fast days of Gedaliah and Esther are not acceptable wedding dates among traditional Jews.

If either the bride or groom becomes a mourner (a designation Halakhicly limited to someone who has lost a mem-

---

* Jews follow a lunar-solar calendar that uses the moon for its basic calculations. The lunar year generally, but not always, has twelve months, which are not aligned with the solar Gregorian calendar.

ber of the immediate family—a parent, chil
spouse), the wedding should be postponed for ι
days following burial. For a parent, the postpoι
be even longer. But in general, the *mitzvah* of
so important that weddings take precedence o
everything else, and in some cases may even
mourning. Your rabbi will be able to advise you should
(God forbid) the situation arise.

Tastes in wedding dates have changed very little over the
centuries. In biblical times weddings were commonly
scheduled in the spring during the month of Adar, when
"the winter is past, the rain is over and gone; the flowers
appear on the earth; the time of singing is come and the
voice of the turtle is heard in our land" (The Song of
Songs).* The autumn was also a popular time for weddings; on the fifteenth of Av—a late summer/early fall
month—the unmarried girls of ancient Israel would dress
in white and go out to sing and dance in the vineyards,
where the young men would follow to seek brides.

For many generations the selection of an auspicious wedding date was of the utmost importance, although customs
varied over centuries and continents. The zodiac was often
consulted in hopes of invoking good spirits and fooling evil
ones. The moon was also shown consideration in setting a
date. It was considered prudent to marry on the new moon,
the first day of the Jewish month, which is celebrated by
the holiday called Rosh Hodesh, or as the moon was wax-
ing in the sky—a symbol of growth and fertility. Some
days of the week were associated with good luck, others
with bad. Monday was generally avoided because in the
Book of Genesis the phrase "and God saw how good this
was" does not appear. On the other hand, Tuesday was

* The Song of Songs—in Hebrew Shir haShirim—is a chapter in the
Bible composed of a collection of wedding hymns. Also called "The
Holy of Holies," these sometimes passionate love poems were interpreted by the rabbis as symbolic of the relationship between God and
the people of Israel.

avored because those words appear twice. The five-day work week has made Sunday the most popular day for scheduling weddings. Saturday-night weddings, the most common choice for formal, evening weddings, usually begin an hour and a half after sunset, to avoid any violation of Shabbat.

The hour of the ceremony is entirely up to you. The later the wedding, the greater the expectation of formality. If you are early risers, an evening ceremony followed by a party that lasts into the wee hours is probably not what you want. Actually, the hour is usually determined by the kind of food you want to serve, the availability of the place you're using, and other basic details. As you plan, take into account the different kinds of energy and emotional connotations of the "seasons" of the day: morning/spring, afternoon/summer, evening/autumn. Or consider choosing a time that the two of you associate with your first meeting or with any important event in your lives together.

There are no laws regarding where a wedding may or may not take place. During the Middle Ages some weddings were even held in cemeteries, since it was believed the life-affirming act of marriage could halt plagues.[4] There are time-honored traditions for holding weddings in the groom's home, in the bride's home, in a social hall or function room, outdoors, and inside a synagogue. Some Orthodox and Hasidic Jews do not marry in a sanctuary, believing that the *huppah*, which symbolizes the marital bedroom (among other things), does not belong near the Ark.

In America today Jewish weddings are most commonly held in synagogues. A sanctuary, especially one in which you have prayed, offers a spirit of *k'dusha*, holiness, in which to start a marriage. The synagogue also provides a link with the larger Jewish community. Since many synagogues have complete kitchen and function-room facilities, many couples choose to have the entire celebration under one roof, not only for the sake of convenience but also to maintain the spirit of the wedding ceremony in the festivities that follow.

Although there are no descriptions of wedding ceremonies in the Bible, a *huppah* under the sky harks back to what was probably biblical custom. Outdoor weddings in a synagogue courtyard became very popular in medieval Europe. Ceremonies were often held in the evenings, the stars shining reminders of God's promise to make Abraham's descendants "as numerous as the stars of heaven" (Genesis 22:17). Today outdoor weddings are still popular, with arboretums, parks, rented estates, and backyards among the sites where *huppot* are raised. If your festivities are going to be held at a hotel and you aren't entirely happy with the décor, layout, or *k'dusha* of the function room at your disposal, it may be possible to arrange an outdoor ceremony on the grounds. (Since outdoor weddings always add anxiety over weather, decide whether rain is something you want to worry about and make contingency plans for.)

Do not procrastinate about finding and booking a location for your wedding. Some popular rental facilities must be reserved more than a year in advance, especially if you're planning on a date in June or September.

Jewish weddings have been sanctified in boathouses and on barges, in catering halls and on beaches. Wherever you are going to marry, spend some time there alone together. If the wedding is going to be held in a park, pick the exact spot and imagine yourselves under a *huppah*, surrounded by family and friends. If you're going to marry in a synagogue, take a few minutes to sit in the sanctuary sometime when it's empty and quiet. It's a very small preparation but one that can help you to savor the upcoming "endlessly precious" hour.

INVITATIONS
AND WEDDING BOOKLETS

For most of Jewish history, weddings were anything but by-invitation-only events. In the *shtetls* of eastern Europe the whole community would be involved in some aspect of the celebration. One went to a wedding (or a *bris*, or a funeral, for that matter) because it was a *mitzvah* to do so —not only for the fun of it but also to fulfill the Talmudic injunction to rejoice with the bride and groom. On many Israeli kibbutzim today the entire community gathers to celebrate the weddings of its members.

Today in America we invite; we make lists, which never include absolutely everyone we want to invite. The size of the guest list is determined by family obligations, money, and decisions about the style of the celebration, and the final list is a composite of as many as four lists: the bride's, the groom's, the bride's parents', and the groom's parents'. Some people try to avoid conflict by setting a fixed numerical limit: the principals invite fifty people each, and that's it.

In theory that's fine, but in practice Judy's family numbers in the dozens, and there's no way to avoid offending all of them without sixty-five invitations. Meanwhile Ben's family includes all of six people, and they're going to feel terribly outnumbered. And since Ben and Judy are paying for half of the wedding, they feel entitled to invite their many friends. Obviously, the final list has to be a compromise that minimizes family strife and maximizes everyone's happiness—or at least satisfaction.

The form of American Jewish wedding invitations has generally conformed to the dictates of secular etiquette. In many cases the only indication on a wedding invitation that anything Jewish is going on is the location of the ceremony and perhaps a family name:

Mr. and Mrs. James Cohen
request the honour of your presence
at the marriage of their daughter
Susan Anna
to
Mr. Harold Green
on Sunday, the sixth of May
at two o'clock
Congregation Beth El
Seventy-five East Street
Mitzvah, Massachusetts
R.S.V.P.

The so-called "traditional Jewish" invitation differs from this Emily Post type invitation only in that Harold's parents in the example above are named right after the Cohens.*

But a wedding invitation can be more than a formulaic announcement of a date, place, and time. It can give your guests a foretaste of the ceremony you're planning and provide hints about the kind of energy that is expected of them. Abandoning the once *de rigueur* high-church tone and British spellings, couples are now creating unique and distinctively Jewish invitations that begin the rejoicing.

Phrasing that departs from standard invitationese is sure to capture guests' imaginations. You needn't be "honoured" to invite people—you can be "pleased" or "happy" or "delighted." Their "participation" might be as important to you as their "presence." You might decide to invite people to "dance at" your wedding rather than just "attend":

* On Israeli invitations the families' names usually appear side by side toward the bottom of the page, identified as "parents of the groom" and "parents of the bride." Side by side or in sequence, it is customary to name the bride's parents first.

Susan Cohen
and
Hal Green
invite you to dance at their wedding
on Sunday, June 15
at two o'clock
Temple Beth El
Mitzvah, Massachusetts

Please reply
_____

Hanna and James Cohen   and   Mary and Al Green
invite you to share
in the joy of their children's wedding
Susan   and   Hal
will meet under the huppah
on Sunday, May 6
at two o'clock
Temple Beth El
Mitzvah, Massachusetts
_____

The joy which the two of us,
Susan Cohen and Hal Green,
give to each other,
we wish to share with our family and friends.
Our parents,
James and Hanna Cohen, of New York City
and
Al and Mary Green, of Orange, New Jersey
invite you to join us in the simcha of our wedding
on Sunday, May 6
at two o'clock
Temple Beth El
Mitzvah, Massachusetts

Many couples and families print the entire invitation
both in English and Hebrew on facing pages, but often the
content of each is quite different. Although Hebrew
names, dates, and phrases now appear more frequently on

the English "side," there are some unique phrases, common to Hebrew invitation texts, that rarely get translated into English. For example, it is traditional to invite guests to attend the wedding "in the streets of Jerusalem, unless the Messiah tarries, in which case the wedding will be held at Congregation Beth Emmet . . ."

Even if neither of you and few of your guests read Hebrew, don't be afraid to use the *aleph-bet*. A transliterated word or a few clearly translated words used in the text or in the graphic design informs your guests that Jewish tradition will be honored at your wedding. And don't worry about confusing people with unfamiliar words; in general, both non-Jews and Jews are far more intrigued than intimidated by the presence of Jewish elements in an invitation.

Susan Anna   *Harold Joseph*
daughter of   *son of*
James and Hanna Cohen   *Al and Mary Green*
invite you to celebrate the simcha of their marriage
on Sunday, June 6, 1984
4 Iyyar 5744
The huppah will be raised at 2 o'clock
Temple Israel
7000 Nachas Road
Smetna, Kansas

To locate your wedding in the flow of Jewish time, you can identify the date on the Jewish calendar either before or after the Gregorian calendar date: "Sunday, June 12, 1983/1 Tammuz 5743." If the date falls on the celebration of the new moon: "Sunday, June 12, 1983/Rosh Chodesh Tammuz 5743." Another way to situate a wedding in Jewish time is to mention the Torah reading closest to your wedding date: "Saturday, August 18, 1984/20 Av 5744, following Shabbat Ekev." For a rather dramatic announcement of the date, a wedding can be described as taking place "5744 years after the creation of the world, Tevet

19." Some Israeli invitations mark time in more secular Jewish terms: "In the 40th year since the creation of the state of Israel."

Finally, recalling the tradition of giving to the poor during times of personal joy and adding to the *mitzvah* of their marriage, some couples add a note requesting that guests make a donation to charity rather than give a wedding gift:

> *We feel that even at an occasion as joyous as a wedding we should remember those in need. Therefore, in lieu of a gift to us, we suggest a gift to one of the following:*
>
> [A list of alternatives is given here.]
>
> *P.S. We would be delighted to accept poems, prose, amulets, mandalas, your thoughts, reminiscences or prognostications, and any other such mementos of the occasion.*

It is very common to use a biblical passage on wedding invitations; some of the most familiar quotations come from the Song of Songs. Probably the most famous of its lines, used in countless invitations, yet somehow always very personal, is "I am my beloved's and my beloved is mine." There are many other appealing phrases, including "This is my beloved, this is my friend." Some passages are especially appropriate for outdoor weddings: "Come my beloved, let us go out to the field," and "You shall go forth in joy and in peace shall you be led. The mountains and hills shall burst into song before you, and all the trees of the field shall applaud." There are also lines that balance male and female imagery: "Like an apple tree among trees of the forest is my beloved among the youths. Like a rose among thorns is my darling among the maidens."

Another common source for quotes is the seven wedding blessings: "You created joy and gladness, bridegroom and bride, mirth and exultation, pleasure and delight"; also

"The voice of joy and the voice of gladness, the voice of the bridegroom and the voice of the bride."

The Torah portion for the week of your wedding might suggest a phrase for the invitation, or consider a brief passage about marriage from the Talmud or the Zohar. Don't feel limited to biblical or liturgical sources.* This story from the Baal Shem Tov makes a wonderful invitation quotation: "From every human being there rises a light that reaches straight to heaven. And when two souls that are destined to be together find each other, their streams of light flow together, and a single brighter light goes forth from their united being."

Design and Calligraphy. Invitations can be engraved or printed by means of thermography, which produces the handsome raised type associated with engraving but at a much lower cost. Invitations can also be offset-printed, photocopied, or even handwritten. Many professional printers offer Hebrew lettering, but if you can't find anyone in your community who does, press-apply Hebrew letters are available at Judaica shops and stationery and graphics-supplies stores. If you're insecure about your use of Hebrew, ask your rabbi or someone who knows the language well to proofread the text before you send it to the printer.

If your *ketubah* is special to you, it might be reproduced and used as the cover design for the invitation. Or the text of your invitation could be printed on the inside of cards purchased at an art museum, gallery, or Judaica store. You might illustrate your own invitation, or an artist friend could design it for you as a wedding gift. And there is no rule that invitations have to be square or rectangular or folded like a book. Indeed, the only applicable Jewish law on the subject of invitations is not even a law but a rabbinic call for *hiddur mitzvah*—the beautification of piety.

* Browse through the wedding poems that begin on page 221 for inspiration.

Jewish symbols lend themselves to all kinds of graphic interpretations: circles and sevens, menorahs and lions, rings and cups, violins and candles, hearts and myrtle branches. The six-pointed star can be incorporated into a mandala design, surrounded by original or quoted poems or prayers. The pomegranate, a biblical symbol of plenty, has decorated wedding invitations, as has the dove, the universal symbol of peace.

The Hebrew *aleph-bet* has a long history of interpretation and embellishment. Happily, there has been a calligraphic renaissance lately, and many talented scribal artists advertise in Jewish newspapers. It's likely that your rabbi can recommend someone. (A *sofer*—a ritual scribe who specializes in the writing of Torah scrolls—may be commissioned to write an invitation and/or a *ketubah*, but his services may be very expensive.)

In addition to having the invitation penned in a fine hand, you might use the services of a good calligrapher who can treat Hebrew letters themselves as design elements. Hebrew names can be calligraphed in the outline of a heart, for example, or the words of a biblical quotation can be penned in a circle, a symbol of union and completion.

Before you settle on a calligrapher, look at a few portfolios; check for consistency in the letters, regularity of spacing between letters and words, and the artist's design sense. When commissioning a calligrapher, make sure you allow enough time for him or her to finish your project. Invitations should be mailed four to six weeks in advance of the wedding, and the calligrapher may need a few months to finish your order, especially if you plan to marry during his/her busy seasons—early summer and autumn. After the artwork is completed, the printer may require another one to three weeks.

Enclosures. The tongue-in-cheek Yiddish-English "translation" for "R.S.V.P." is "Remember to Send Vedding Presents." This formal abbreviation or simply "Please reply" should be sufficient reminder for guests to respond. However, it has become customary to enclose a reply card ("M———will/will not attend") and a self-addressed, stamped envelope to ensure an answer. Etiquette mavens uniformly decry this development as proof of the laziness of wedding guests, who apparently don't voluntarily write the formal little reply notes they used to. It also adds an additional expense for the hosts. One alternative is to include a self-addressed postcard that says only "Please respond." Not only does this minimize postage costs a bit, but some of the replies will be priceless and maybe even fuel for the fire of a master of ceremonies.*

If some wedding guests are invited to cocktails only and others invited to dinner,† various enclosures need to be included in the envelope. Or you may want to enclose some information that doesn't fit in with the tone of your invitation—perhaps directions to the synagogue and motel rates. If there is going to be a special *Oneg Shabbat* (an informal meal after Friday-evening services) or an *aufruf* (recognition of the groom—and bride—by calling them up to the Torah during Shabbat morning services), you might include a Xeroxed or offset-printed note inviting people to attend. (Family dinners generally don't require a written invitation.) And if you're planning a participatory celebration in which the bride and groom are treated—as tradition dictates—like a queen and king, you can ask your guests to come prepared to entertain you with jokes, reminiscences, magic tricks, poems, juggling routines, songs, dances, and happy hearts.

Wedding Booklets. Many couples are nervous about the amount of Hebrew and English or the proportion of He-

* See section "Laughter, Music, and Dance."
† For the wedding and reception or dinner to require separate invitations is in itself not very Jewish. When the glass has been shattered and the guests cry "Mazel tov!" the wedding is only half over. According to tradition, feasting and merrymaking are an integral part of Jewish weddings, and if that means there has to be a less lavish spread, so be it.

I AM MY
BELOVED'S
AND MY
BELOVED IS MINE

Two Invitation Covers

Two designs: © Jonathan Kremer

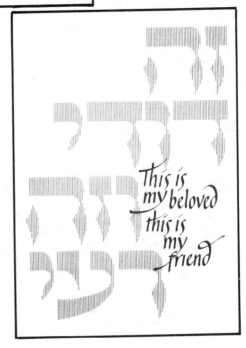

This is my beloved this is my friend

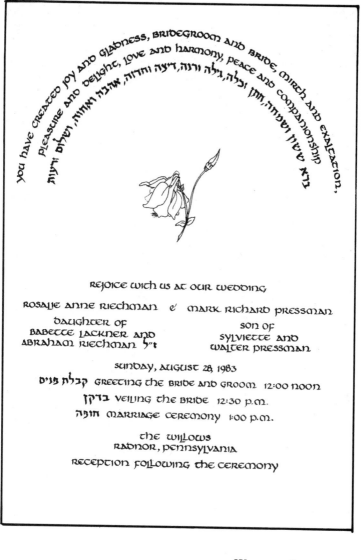

you have created joy and gladness, bridegroom and bride, mirth and exultation, pleasure and delight, love and harmony, peace and companionship

אשר ברא ששון ושמחה, חתן וכלה, גילה רנה, דיצה וחדוה, אהבה ואחוה, ושלום ורעות

REJOICE WITH US AT OUR WEDDING

ROSALIE ANNE RIECHMAN & MARK RICHARD PRESSMAN

DAUGHTER OF   SON OF
BABETTE LACKNER AND   SYLVIETTE AND
ABRAHAM RIECHMAN ז״ל   WALTER PRESSMAN

SUNDAY, AUGUST 28, 1983
קבלת פנים GREETING THE BRIDE AND GROOM 12:00 NOON
בדקן VEILING THE BRIDE 12:30 P.M.
חופה MARRIAGE CEREMONY 1:00 P.M.

THE WILLOWS
RADNOR, PENNSYLVANIA
RECEPTION FOLLOWING THE CEREMONY

WEDDING INVITATION

Design and Calligraphy © Susan Leviton

ברוך ה׳ אלהי ישראל אמן

Rabbi and Mrs. David J. Jacobs
request your presence
at the marriage of their daughter
Abigail Judith
to
Daniel
son of Dr. Michael and Dr. Edith Wyschogrod
Sunday, June twentieth, at one o'clock
Temple Beth El
One-thousand-one Hancock Street
Quincy, Massachusetts   RSVP

השתתפות כבודכם מתבקשת
כאשר יכנסו לחופה
החתן דניאל נ״י
בן דר׳ יעקב מיכאל ודר חיה שרה וישוגרוד
עם כלתו אביגיל יהודית שתח׳
בת הרב דוד יוסף והרבנית צפורה צביה יעקבי
אחד בשבת פרשת קרח
עשרים ותשעה ימים לחדש סיון
שנת שי׳מי כחותם על לבך
בית כנסת בית אל, קווינזי

ולא נמצא מכלם כדניאל

והאשה טובת שכל ויפת תאר

WEDDING INVITATION

INVITATION COVER

© *Susan Leviton*

WEDDING INVITATION, COVER AND TEXT

© *Claire Mendelson*

בעזהש"ת

We join our parents in inviting you to the celebration of our wedding. It will take place, please G-d, on Sunday, the twelfth of August, 1979, the nineteenth day of Av, 5739, at Lincoln Square Synagogue, Amsterdam Avenue and Sixty-Ninth Street, New York City. The Chupah will begin at six o'clock in the evening. We look forward to greeting you at cocktails and dinner afterward. Your participation will enhance our joy and the meaning of the occasion.

Geraldine and Isaac

R.S.V.P. before
July 18

brew to English in their wedding ceremony. Will too much Hebrew confuse or alienate people who are unfamiliar with the language? Will too much English offend more traditional members of the family and/or make the ceremony feel watered-down to the point of Protestantism?

There should be enough English so that everyone understands what is taking place. The rabbis who wrote the Talmud believed that thorough comprehension of the terms of marriage was so important that they ruled that key parts of the ceremony be repeated in the everyday language of the bride and groom. However, to make Hebrew incidental to the service weakens its power. Not only does the language contain nuances absent in the English, it places the *huppah* in the context of history, the history of a particular family within the context of the history of the people of Israel. Besides, clearly translated Hebrew does not alienate anyone. Non-Hebrew-speaking guests are generally delighted to learn.

Couples who reclaim and reinterpret Jewish wedding tradition often find that words and customs that have become second nature to them are unfamiliar to their families and friends. In order to explain and put people at ease, many couples are providing a sort of "program" for their guests—a guidebook-glossary to the events of their day.

Wedding booklets can contain everything from your *ketubah* text to acknowledgments of the musicians and caterer. Some couples write a letter welcoming their guests and inviting their participation, others have included prayers for responsive reading during the wedding, definitions of terms (not everyone knows what a *huppah* is) and explanations of customs such as *mikvah* and *yichud*, historical background, and a step-by-step guide to the ceremony.

The booklet can be simple or elaborate. It can consist of a single photocopied sheet of paper or a pamphlet of many pages, bound and printed on glossy paper. It can be typed or calligraphed, decorated or plain. For the cover, couples have reproduced the design of their wedding invitation or their *ketubah*. Not only is the booklet a meaningful part of the day, it serves as a kind of "souvenir," though on rather a higher spiritual plane than monographed matchbooks or cocktail napkins.

This "new" custom is really only a variation on an old practice. Jewish weddings have long featured a booklet called a *bencher* from the word *benchen*, or prayer. (*Benchen* —or *benching*—refers specifically to praying the *birkhat hamazon* after meals.) *Benchers* contain *birkhat hamazon*, the blessings after meals, and the seven marriage blessings, which are repeated after eating. (See "Concluding the Festivities" for more on *benching* and *benchers*.)

WEDDING CLOTHES, WEDDING RINGS

. . . God has dressed me with garments of exultation, . . . As a bridegroom puts on a priestly diadem, And as a bride adorns herself with her jewels.

Isaiah 61:10

While priestly diadems are rarely part of wedding costumes these days, the attire and adornment of brides and grooms remain as important as they were in biblical times. The common panic over finding the "perfect" dress or shoes or suit is not merely an exercise in vanity. No matter how simple, wedding clothes are the most important ritual garments most of us will ever own. Although the rabbis of the Talmud warned against excessive displays of finery at weddings, so as to spare the feelings of poor relatives, the traditional image of the bridal couple as king and queen invites elegance and display.

There are no Halakhic or legal requirements regarding

dress other than the injunction that clothes be both modest and attractive—which leaves a great deal to personal taste and contemporary style. Paintings, drawings, and descriptions of Jewish bridal costumes throughout history demonstrate that Jews have always been influenced by local fashion. While Ashkenazic brides wore the white gown and lacy veil common to European Christian weddings, Sephardic brides donned bright, colorful costumes, their veils often decorated with a cascade of gold coins, similar to the garments of their Muslim neighbors. Grooms' fashions varied similarly.

There is, however, one religious imperative that has too long been neglected, from Minsk to Morocco to Michigan. The *mitzvah*/obligation of rejoicing at a wedding is incumbent on the bride and groom as well as on the guests. Anything that gets in the way of the bride's or groom's happiness—from a too-tight waist to uncomfortable shoes to someone else's idea of "appropriate"—is worse than a nuisance. It's a sin! Whatever you wear, it should make *you* feel attractive, regal, and terrific.

Although Jewish law is quite relaxed about wedding apparel, there are some sartorial customs that have attained the force of law. One of these is the wearing of bridal white. In Jewish practice the wearing of white has as much to do with spiritual purity as physical virginity. A wedding is considered a personal Yom Kippur, a day of repentance and forgiveness for the couple. Among Orthodox Jews the bride's white dress indicates that she has been to *mikvah*, the ritual bath, in preparation for the wedding, and the groom's *kittel* (a short white linen robe—something like a pharmacist's coat—bound by a white belt and worn over his suit) represents his spiritual readiness for marriage.

In traditional practice a veil is always part of the bride's attire as a reminder of Rebekah's action and as a symbol of modesty. (In Genesis, Rebekah "took the veil and covered herself" when she first saw Isaac, her husband-to-be.) The shape and size of the veil match the style of the wedding dress, and a headdress of some sort is customary. The ancient use of crowns to celebrate the "royalty" of the bridal pair is still echoed in the use of a tiara or a floral garland to anchor the veil. Some liberal Jews do not attach much importance to the veil and have dispensed with it. Some women dislike its associations with Middle Eastern *purdah*, the heavy covering of married women, but others claim that the veil is the one piece of clothing that makes them feel set apart and uniquely "bridal."

A groom dons the *kittel* just before entering the *huppah* and removes it after the wedding ceremony is over. *Kittels* can be purchased at Judaica shops or easily made by using a bathrobe pattern or elongating a shirt pattern. The belt should be made of the same material as the garment.[5] Wearing the *kittel* is an Ashkenazic custom. Sephardic grooms sometimes wrap themselves and their brides in a single large *tallis* (prayer shawl) during the wedding ceremony, creating an intimate *huppah* beneath the *huppah*.

While the bride's veil is traditionally worn only once, a *kittel* is worn on special ritual occasions throughout life: on Yom Kippur, at Passover seders, and, finally, as a shroud. Recently some women have turned parts of their wedding attire—a short veil, a white shawl, *tallis*, simple white dress, or even a bridal *kittel*—into ritual garments that are also worn at religiously significant moments, which might include the *brit* (covenant) celebration of a child.

Wedding Rings. In Jewish law a verbal declaration of marriage is not legally binding in and of itself. There must be also an act of *kinyan*—a formal, physical acquisition. Without the groom's giving and the bride's acceptance of some object of nominal value—something *shaveh p'rutah*, literally, "worth a penny"—there is no marriage. Since the seventh century a ring has been the traditional and preferred object of exchange.

According to Jewish law the ring must be unpierced and

free of precious stones to avoid any possible misrepresentation of its value. The ring should belong to the groom, although he may borrow one if the bride is aware he has done so.[6] Only one ring—given by the groom to the bride —is required by law. Believing that an exchange of rings invalidates the *kinyan*, some traditional rabbis refuse to perform double-ring ceremonies. Liberal rabbis usually incorporate the bride's gift of a ring to the groom in the ceremony.

For the most part, Jewish wedding rings are extremely simple pieces of jewelry. Even in the European communities of the sixteenth and seventeenth centuries in Europe, when large, ornate marriage rings decorated with the towers of the Temple in Jerusalem were lent to the bridal couple for their wedding celebrations, a simple ring was later substituted for everyday use.

A band made of a single pure metal, with no holes breaking the circle, represents the wholeness achieved through marriage and a hope for an unbroken union. The circle is an ancient symbol common to many cultures. In various times and places it has been a sign of perfection, completion, safety, and the female. The mystics who wrote the Zohar perceived the ring as a circle of light that revealed the "enveloping" sexual mystery of marriage.[7]

While simple gold bands remain the traditional and most popular choice, embellishment with Hebrew letters has come back into fashion. It was once common for the words, *mazel tov*—good luck—to be engraved inside the ring. More popular today is the declaration "Dodi Li V' Ani Lo" ("I am my beloved's and my beloved is mine"), which is sometimes rendered in gold filigree on the ring. A few jewelers have created special designs specifically for Jewish weddings. Your rabbi might be able to suggest such a local craftsperson, or you can ask at a Judaica shop. Many goldsmiths will make rings to customers' specifications.[8] Hebrew names and/or the Jewish date of the wedding can be engraved inside by most jewelers.

THE *KETUBAH*

To the Midrashic imagination, the whole Torah is a *ketubah*—a marriage contract—between God and the people of Israel. But for American Jews of the past few generations the *ketubah* was often little more than a formality. The rabbi generally supplied a printed document and explained its historical and Halakhic significance to the bride and groom. It would be signed in the rabbi's study or on a corner of a banquet table, sometimes read during the ceremony, and then filed away along with the secular marriage certificate, more or less forgotten. Some early Reform rabbis even ignored the tradition of the *ketubah* altogether. Recently the *ketubah* has experienced a revival. Once again it has become a source of inspiration for artists and calligraphers. And, most important, for many couples it has become a Jewish focal point in their wedding preparations.[9]

Tradition. The *ketubah* is one of the oldest and one of the least romantic elements of Jewish weddings. It is a legal contract, pure and simple. In its traditional form the *ketubah* does not mention love or trust or the establishment of a Jewish home or even God. It is written in Aramaic, "the technical, legal language of talmudic law, rather than in Hebrew, the language of the Song of Songs."[10]

A traditional *ketubah* is not a contract between bride and groom but a document signed by two witnesses who testify that the groom "acquired" the bride in the prescribed manner and that he agreed to support her. This is not a mutual agreement; the bride only has to willingly accept the groom's proposal of marriage. The *ketubah* is given to the bride as a surety of her rights and her husband's duties; it becomes her (not their) possession.

The *ketubah* is considered a great advance for its time (the end of the first century, C.E.) because it provided women with legal status and rights in marriage. It is also credited with strengthening the Jewish family since it made divorce —otherwise an easily exercised male prerogative—costly. Since the second century, rabbis held that without a *ketubah* "the union of husband and wife was unhallowed cohabitation,"[11] and it remained a crucial document for many generations.* In 1306, when Jews were stripped of their belongings and expelled from France, the rabbinic authorities declared that until new *ketubot* were delivered to the wives, there could be no conjugal relations.[12]

While *ketubot* have been written on all kinds of paper and ornamented in countless ways, changes in the text have been relatively rare. Some Sephardic *ketubot* embellished the names of the principals with long lists of honorifics: ". . . the bridegroom, who bears the good, resplendent name, the perspicacious, the wise, of holy seed, the honorable Abraham, a pure Sephardi, the son of the honorable, who bears a good name, the exalted gentleman, the uplifted one in name and praise, the wise and perspicacious one, of holy seed, the honoured Rabbi and teacher Isaac . . ."[13] During perilous times *ketubot* included special pledges by the groom not to take "adventurous voyages or to expose himself to the risks of travellers and traders."[14]

By and large, however, variations in the *ketubah* are insignificant compared with the extent to which the text has remained constant. The traditional document still in use shares a great deal with marriage contracts from the second century, C.E. (An example of the modern Orthodox *ketubah* appears at the end of this chapter.)

New Ketubot. Although it was a great advance for its time, the traditional *ketubah* does not address the realities of life

---

* Despite the Halakhic insistence on a *ketubah*, it also recognizes common-law marriage. If witnesses testify that a Jewish couple is living together as husband and wife, a *bet din*, a court of rabbis, would consider the traditional *ketubah* to be in effect.

for men and women today. It is very difficult for many couples and rabbis to use the traditional text and then affirm, as is also traditional, that the *ketubah* is not to be regarded as an *ashakhta*—"a mere formula." The elaborate economic arrangements for the dissolution of a marriage as spelled out in a traditional *ketubah* have become meaningless, and the changed aspirations, roles, and responsibilities of women and men find no expression in a contract that demands specific duties and responsibilities of the groom but asks the bride for nothing in return.

Since the early 1970s, and especially since the publication of a sample "equalized *ketubah*" in the *First Jewish Catalog*, brides and grooms, rabbis and calligraphers have been experimenting with new *ketubot*. One rabbi has called these documents *brit ketubot*—"covenant *ketubot*"—an expression that acknowledges the difference between these new contracts and traditional *ketubot* and also emphasizes the seriousness and mutuality of an agreement to marry.[15]

Many new *ketubot* include two parallel declarations of commitment made by the bride and groom, followed by a joint affirmation of the couple's connection to God, Torah, *mitzvot*, and to the Jewish people. (See examples at end of chapter.) Whatever the form or content, it's best for the text to be simple and brief. Generally these *ketubot* are written and signed both in English and Hebrew. If you aren't fluent in Hebrew, a rabbi or Hebrew-speaking friend can help translate your English text. These *ketubot* are commonly signed by the bride and groom, by two witnesses, and the rabbi.

Jewish law recognizes the validity of the traditional *ketubah* only, so some couples choose to have both a traditional and a *brit ketubah*. There have also been efforts to write *ketubot* that are both egalitarian and Halakhicly acceptable. As long as the basic requirements spelled out in the Torah are met, additions to the text (clearly visible as such) are not strictly forbidden (see example). In line with this approach, some couples choose to have four witnesses sign

KETUBAH

KETUBAH

KETUBAH

© 1982 Elly Simmons

KETUBAH

Design: Lesley Rubin. Calligraphy: Jonathan Kremer

KETUBAH

© Claire Mendelson

KETUBAH

© *"Garden of Israel" Ketubab, limited edition serigraph print: Shonna Husbands-Hankin*

KETUBAH

Miriam Karp

their *ketubot*. The signatures of two observant Jewish males are required, but since the addition of other names is not specifically forbidden, two women are also asked to sign.

Hiddur Mitzvah. Unlike the writing of a Torah scroll or other ritual documents, there are relatively few requirements for the lettering or form of a *ketubah*. But according to the rabbinic principle of *hiddur mitzvah*, when a physical object is needed to fulfill a commandment, the object should be made as beautiful as possible. The *ketubah* has been lovingly and variously interpreted and decorated through the generations.

The earliest known decorated *ketubah* dates from the tenth century, and illustrated and illuminated *ketubot* have been produced by Jews all over the world ever since, in styles reflecting the tastes of nations and epochs. The Jews of Persia made *ketubot* that seem to float on magic Oriental carpets, and North African Jews surrounded the text with the intricate geometrical shapes that adorned the mosques of their Moslem neighbors. The Italian *ketubot* of the seventeenth and eighteenth centuries are especially elaborate, alive with birds, flowers, signs of the Zodiac, representations of biblical lovers and even pagan gods and goddesses.

Modern *ketubot* are decorated with techniques ranging from paper-cutting to lithography to silk-screening to watercolor. If you or a friend have artistic abilities, you might create a "frame," or environment, in which a calligrapher can write the text. Or if you find a work of art that is especially meaningful, a large mat around it can be lettered with the *ketubah* text. It is considered a great *mitzvah* to write your own *ketubah*, and there are books that provide step-by-step guides to English and Hebrew calligraphy for do-it-yourselfers.[16]

The professionally calligraphed *ketubah* is currently very popular. There are calligraphers in many cities who write and illustrate *ketubot*. Check Jewish periodicals for advertisements and ask your rabbi to suggest some artists. As

ıg a calligrapher for a wedding invitation, try
: work of a few artists before making a decision.
s long as three months to commission an origi-
so plan ahead. You should be aware that com-
ı calligraphed *ketubah* can be very expensive.
Some of the illuminated and/or gold-leaf-lettered documents run into thousands of dollars. There are, however,
more and more lovely lithographs and prints becoming
available at reasonable rates.*

It's easy to get caught up in the process of shopping for
the most beautiful *ketubah* you can find. Some couples,
however, choose to write their marriage contract simply,
without embellishment, on plain paper. The *ketubot* of poor
east European Jews who fled pogroms and persecution
were often irregularly lettered onto coarse brown paper.
Yet some of these rough documents that survived time and
steerage are far more moving than the illuminated Italian
masterpieces preserved in museums.

Afterward. Traditionally, the *ketubah* becomes the property of the bride after the wedding. In Persia, women kept
ketubot under their pillows, carefully folded inside silk envelopes. Many couples frame and hang their *ketubot* in special places in their homes. If you shared the same bed
before marriage, hanging the *ketubah* over it affirms the
change in your relationship.

The Baal Shem Tov said that if a couple was fighting,
they should read the *ketubah* aloud to each other because
this would help them remember the day of their marriage,
when they affirmed their covenant with each other, when
they were surrounded with love and good wishes, and
when God entered their relationship.[17]

* The names and addresses of a number of calligraphers appear on
p. 245–46.

SAMPLE *KETUBOT*

ORTHODOX *Ketubah*

On the ____ day of the week, the ____ day of the month ____ in the year five thousand seven hundred and ____ since the creation of the world according to the reckoning which we are accustomed to use here in the city of _____ in _____. That _____ son of _____ of the family _____ said to this maiden _____ daughter of _____ of the family _____, "Be my wife according to the law of Moses and Israel, and I will cherish, honor, support, and maintain you in accordance with the custom of Jewish husbands, who cherish, honor, support, and maintain their wives faithfully. And I here present you with the marriage gift of virgins, two hundred silver zuzim, which belongs to you, according to the law of Moses and Israel; and I will also give you your food, clothing, and necessities, and live with you as husband and wife according to the universal custom." And _____, this maiden consented and became his wife. The trousseau that she brought to him from her father's house in silver, gold, valuables, clothing, furniture, and bedclothes, all this _____, the bridegroom accepted in the sum of one hundred silver pieces, and _____ the bridegroom consented to increase this amount from his own property with the sum of one hundred silver pieces, making in all two hundred silver pieces. And thus said _____ the bridegroom, "The responsibility of this marriage contract, of this trousseau, and of this additional sum, I take upon myself and my heirs after me, so that they shall be paid from the best part of my property and possessions that I have beneath the whole heaven, that which I now possess or may hereafter acquire. All my property, real and personal, even the shirt from my back, shall be mortgaged to secure the payment of this marriage contract, of the trous-

seau, and of the addition made to it, during my lifetime and after my death, from the present day and
forever." _____ the bridegroom, has taken upon
himself the responsibility of this marriage contract, of
the trousseau and the addition made to it, according to
the restrictive usages of all marriage contracts and the
additions to them made for the daughters of Israel,
according to the institutions of our sages of blessed
memory. It is not to be regarded as an indecisive con-
tractual obligation or as a mere formula of a document.
We have followed the legal formality of symbolic delivery (kinyan) between _____ son of _____ and
_____ daughter of _____ this maiden and we have
used a garment legally fit for the purpose, to
strengthen all that is stated above,

AND EVERYTHING IS VALID
AND CONFIRMED.

Attested to _____ Witness
Attested to _____ Witness

TRADITIONAL-EGALITARIAN *Ketubah*

On _____ in the year five thousand seven hundred
and ___ since the creation of the world, according to
the reckoning which we use here in _____ We
witness that the bridegroom _____ said to the
maiden _____, "Be my wife according to the law of
Moses and Israel, and I will work for, honor, support,
and maintain you in accordance with the custom of
Jewish husbands who serve, honor, support, and
maintain their wives in truth. And I will give you the
dowry of your maidenhood 200 zuz (pieces of silver)
in case, God forbid, that I give you a divorce or in
case, God forbid, I should die, to which you are entitled by the law of the Torah and also your food, clothing, and all your needs and I will live with you
according to the universal custom." And the maiden
_____ consented and became his wife. And the

bridegroom _____ said, "The responsibility for this marriage contract I take upon myself and my heirs after me, to be paid from the best and the choicest of my properties and of my possessions that I have beneath the whole heaven anywhere that I now possess or may ever acquire; my property, real and personal, shall serve as warranty and security for the payment of this marriage contract, from me and even from the garment on my shoulders, during my lifetime and after my death, from this day forever." The responsibility of this marriage contract has been taken upon himself by the bridegroom _____ according to the restrictive usages of all marriage contracts for the daughters of Israel, according to the institutions of our sages.

We witness that the woman _____ said to her husband _____, "I am my beloved's and my beloved is mine. And I pledge that I will work for, support, honor, and maintain you and will provide your food, clothing, and needs at any time and every time that we mutually agree. That I will work for, support, and provide for our family as the principal provider, or at any time that you may be unable to work for and support me and our family due to any injury or accident or disability that might occur to you in the future. And I will live with you as is the way of the world. And _____ consented and became her husband. Further, the woman pledged and said, "In the event, God forbid, there is a divorce while I am the principal family provider, I will give you an additional sum of 400 zuz." And the woman _____ said, "The responsibility for this ketubah, this additional sum, I take upon myself to be paid from the best and choicest of the moveable possessions that I have under heaven, that I now possess or may ever acquire; my moveable property, real and personal, shall serve as warranty and security for the payment of this ketubah, this additional sum from me and even from the garment on my shoulders, during my lifetime and after my death, from this day forever." The responsibility of this ketubah and additional sum has been taken upon herself by the woman _____ according to the restrictive usages of all customary ketubot, according to the institution of our sages.

And the groom and bride have also promised each other to strive throughout their lives together to achieve an openness which will enable them to share their thoughts, their feelings, and their experiences, to be sensitive at all times to each others' needs, to attain mutual intellectual, emotional, physical, and spiritual fulfillment, to work for the perpetuation of Judaism and of the Jewish people in their home, in their family life, and in their communal endeavors.

This contract is not to be considered a non-serious obligation or as mere form. And we have received a token of acquisition from the groom _____ to the bride _____ and from the woman _____ to her husband _____ regarding all that has been written and explained above, that is a valid token for acquisition.

All is valid and binding.

_____ Witness
_____ Witness
_____ Witness
_____ Witness

The above *ketubah*, coauthored by Rabbi Joel Schwab, is intended as "a marriage contract that includes all the elements required by Jewish law while at the same time attempting to make the *ketubah* egalitarian." The elements commanded in the Torah are all here: the groom's pledge to provide the bride with food and clothing and his pledge of a sum to be paid in case of divorce or death. But since the *ketubah* may also contain agreements above and beyond this, the bride voluntarily assumes a number of specific responsibilities that parallel the groom's. Since they are not

Halakhicly defined, these additions can take any form. Thus the following paragraph could appear alongside or after this or another traditional text:

We have learned by study that the basic principle of Jewish marriage is that husband and wife take equal responsibility for entering into and maintaining their marriage. For it is written (Baba Kama 15a): "Scripture has made man and woman equal with regard to all the Laws of the Torah." Thus when _____, this woman, consented and became his wife, she did so by saying to _____, "I will. And be thou my husband according to the Law of Moses and Israel and I will work for you according to the custom of Jewish wives who work for their husbands, and honor, support, and maintain them in truth. And I will provide your food, clothing, and necessities which belong to you according to the law of Moses and will live with you in conjugal relations according to universal custom. And to this _____, the bridegroom said, "I will." _____ and _____ each contributed valuable property to the marriage and pledged their spiritual and emotional resources to its maintenance. They exchanged gold rings that each might carry a symbol of this pledge and of their love for each other.

New *Ketubot*

On the _____ day of the week the _____ day of _____ five thousand seven hundred _____ since the creation of the world as we reckon time here in _____.

The bride _____ daughter of _____ and _____ promised _____ the groom, son of _____ and _____ You are my husband according to the tradition of Moses and Israel. I shall cherish you and honor you as is customary among the daughters of Israel who have cherished and honored their husbands in faithfulness and in integrity.

The groom _____ son of _____ and _____ promised _____ the bride, daughter of _____ and _____ You are my wife according to the tradition of Moses and Israel. I shall cherish you and honor you as is customary among the sons of Israel who have cherished and honored their wives in faithfulness and in integrity.

The groom and bride have also promised each other to strive throughout their lives together to achieve an openness which will enable them to share their thoughts, their feelings, and their experiences.

To be sensitive at all times to each others' needs, to attain mutual intellectual, emotional, physical, and spiritual fulfillment. To work for the perpetuation of Judaism and of the Jewish people in their home, in their family life, and in their communal endeavors.

This marriage has been authorized also by the civil authorities of _____.

It is valid and binding.

Witness _____   Witness _____

Bride _____   Groom _____
Rabbi _____

This *ketubah*, written by Rabbi Bernard H. Mehlman, Rabbi Gustav Buchdahl, and Rabbi Eugene R. Lipman and widely circulated throughout the 1970s, has served as a model for countless marriage contracts. Rabbi Lawrence Kushner, who calligraphed the *ketubah*, designed its innovative and much-copied two-column format.[18]

The following three *ketubot* only suggest the variety of marriage contracts being written today.

On the first day toward Shabbat, the _____ day of _____, in the year five thousand seven hundred and _____ since the creation of the world according to our accustomed reckoning in _____, _____ [bride's name] and _____ [groom's name], in the presence of beloved family and friends entered into this covenant with each other.

We promise to consecrate ourselves, one to the other as husband and wife, according to the tradition of Moses and Israel; to love, honor, and cherish each other; to work together to create a home faithful to the teachings of Torah, reverent of the Divine, and committed to deeds of loving-kindness. We promise to try always to bring out in ourselves and in each other qualities of forgiveness, compassion, and integrity. All this we take upon ourselves to uphold to the best of our abilities.

Groom _____
Bride _____

By means of the traditional symbolic transfer, *kinyan*, we have affirmed the mutual agreement of the bride and groom. All this is confirmed and abiding.

Witness _____
Witness _____

●

On the first day of the week of the portion Ekev on the _____ day of the month of Av in the year _____ since the creation of the world according to our accustomed reckoning in the city of _____, corresponding to _____ 198 ___,

In accordance with the laws of Moses and the people Israel, we _____ and _____ stand under the *huppah* before family and friends to make a mutual covenant as husband and wife, partners in marriage.

Together we will build a home as a sanctuary of peace shared with the community of Israel; guided by a reverence for the Divine, the teachings of Torah and good deeds, and linked eternally to the history of our ancestors and to the future of the Jewish people.

We, as beloveds and friends, promise to give each other joy and support one another in sadness, to cherish our differences, to strengthen one another in our goals, and to bring up our children within the covenant of Israel.

And everything is valid and confirmed.

Attested to by _____ witness
Attested to by _____ witness
Groom _____
Bride _____

●

On the _____ day of the week the _____ day of _____ five thousand seven hundred _____ years since the creation of the world as we reckon here in __

The bride _____ daughter of _____ & _____ says to the groom, "With this ring you are consecrated unto me as my husband according to the tradition of Moses and the Jewish people. I shall treasure you, nourish you, support you, and respect you as Jewish women have devoted themselves to their husbands with integrity."

The groom _____ son of _____ & _____ says to the bride, "With this ring you are consecrated unto me as my wife according to the tradition of Moses and the Jewish people. I shall treasure you, nourish you, support you, and respect you as Jewish men have devoted themselves to their wives with integrity."

We promise to try to be ever open to one another while cherishing each other's uniqueness; to comfort and challenge each other through life's sorrow and joy; to share our intuition and insight with one another; and above all to do everything within our power to permit each of us to become the persons we are yet to be.

We also pledge to establish a home open to the spiritual potential in all life; a home wherein the flow of the seasons and the passages of life are celebrated through the symbols of our Jewish heritage; a home filled with reverence for learning, loving, and generosity; a home wherein ancient melody, candles, and wine sanctify the table; a home joined ever more closely to the community of Israel.

This marriage has been authorized also by the civil authorities of _____. It is valid and binding.

Witness _____   Witness _____

Bride _____   Groom _____
Rabbi _____

The text of this *ketubah* was written by Rabbi Gustav Buchdahl, Rabbi Lawrence Kushner, and Rabbi Bernard H. Mehlman.[19]

THE *HUPPAH*

The bridal canopy is a multifaceted symbol: it is a home, a garment, a bedcovering, and a reminder of the tents of nomadic ancestors. The fact that the *huppah* is open on all sides recalls in particular the tent of Abraham, the paragon of hospitality, who had doors on all four sides of his dwelling so that visitors would always know they were welcome.

In Talmudic times the groom's father set up a royal purple tent in the courtyard of his home where the marriage would be finalized by consummation. Over time, *nissuin* became a symbolic act, which the groom accomplished by covering the bride with a garment—a veil or his *tallis*—and the word *huppah* became identified with the act of "covering" or "taking" the bride.[20]

Long after tents vanished from the Jewish landscape,

wedding ceremonies were held out of doors in the hope that the marriage would be blessed by as many children as "the stars of the heavens." Some kind of covering was employed to create a more modest and sanctified space, separated from the "marketplace." During the sixteenth century, probably in Poland, a portable canopy held aloft by four poles came into vogue, and over time the word *huppah* became identified more with this canopy than with its legal function of *nissuin*.

The Midrashists wrote that God created ten splendid *huppot* for the marriage of Adam and Eve. And the tabernacle built by the Israelites in the desert is also described as a bridal canopy.[21] In some European communities richly embroidered arc coverings *(parochet)* were used for weddings, but many couples married under a *tallis*, which was frequently a gift from the bride or her family to the groom. The *tallis tzitzit* (ritual fringes) hanging above the couple's heads were regarded as talismans against evil spirits. According to Gematria, a numerical system in which every Hebrew letter has a numerical value, the thirty-two bunches of *tzitzit* mystically correspond to the total achieved by the Hebrew word for heart, which is *lev*.

The *huppah* is understood as a sign of God's presence at the wedding and in the home being established under the canopy. *Huppah* means "that which covers or floats above." It is said that the space beneath the canopy is spiritually charged because the divine Name floats above it.

The Canopy. The *huppah* should be a temporary, handmade structure. Trees do not count, nor are *huppot* made entirely of flowers strictly kosher. Despite the fact that the canopy has a legal function, there are no Halakhic requirements about its dimensions, shape, or decoration. Its appearance is entirely a matter of taste, another opportunity for personal expression and *hiddur mitzvah*—the beautification of piety.

Many synagogues own *huppot* they make available to

marrying couples. Some of these are quite be
broidered or woven with quotations from the
ding blessings and decorated with familiar imag
cups, doves, and scenes of Jerusalem. Synag(
tend to be stationary structures that are set up o
in advance of the ceremony.

And recently the use of a *tallis* as a canopy has made a
comeback. Marrying under *tzitzit*, which are reminders of
the *mitzvot*, is seen as an affirmation of the couple's commitment to a shared Jewish life. Obviously, in order to
function as a *huppah*, a *tallis* needs to be a full-sized garment, one that covers two-thirds of the body, not the "bi-
kini" *tallesim* worn by many b'nai and b'not mitzvah. One
couple used the prayer shawl of a beloved grandfather, who
had carried his *tallis* from Poland to America fifty years
earlier.

For people with the time and inclination, making a *huppah* can be a very satisfying project. Special talents are not
necessary to create something of meaning. You can simply
buy a special piece of fabric in colors and a pattern you
particularly like (three feet by five feet is a good size) and
hem it. A *huppah* can be batiked, silk-screened, woven,
appliquéd, or embroidered. Many needlecraft and embroi-
dery books feature patterns that can be traced or ironed
onto the fabric. (Judaica shops generally carry tablecloth
patterns that can be adapted for use on a *huppah*.) The
American friendship quilt has inspired some women to create individual squares that are then sewn together for the
canopy.

For those who don't sew, words can be calligraphed or
patterns hand-painted on fabric. Colorful pieces of felt can
be cut and pasted in any shape or pattern. Or the *huppah*
can be created at a prewedding party at which guests inscribe blessings onto a plain piece of canvas or linen with a
rainbow of watercolor pens. One couple used this occasion
to teach their friends some of the songs that were to be sung
at the wedding.

The seven marriage blessings have inspired many *huppah* designs. Among the best known of these images is the "rejoicing voices": "Kol sasson v'kol simcha, kol kallah v'kol hatan" ("The voice of joy and the voice of gladness, the voice of the bride and the voice of the bridegroom"). Other traditional subjects suggested by the *sheva b'rachot* include the two cups of wine, Eden, and the streets of Jerusalem. The stars and the moon are often pictured on *huppot* as portents of children to come.[22] But there is no rule that the *huppah* must be covered with publicly recognizable images and symbols. One bride and groom, who over many years had collected frog and elephant memorabilia, incorporated their "mascots" in a scene of Jerusalem.

When planning a *huppah* cover, make sure to provide some means of hanging it securely from four poles. Eyelets, curtain rings, or clasps should be fastened to the canopy so there is no danger of its slipping during the ceremony. *Tallesim* are easily hung from the long loops that attach the fringes.

The poles should be long enough—four or five feet at least—to ensure the comfort of your *huppah* bearers during the ceremony. Wooden dowels, available at most lumberyards, can easily be cut to length, and bamboo is both lightweight and pretty. Wood can be carved and/or painted; ribbons, colored masking tape, crepe paper, flowers, and greenery can be used for decoration.

According to one custom, parents would plant a cypress tree on the birth of a son and a cedar on the birth of a daughter. At the time of the children's marriage, branches from each would be cut and carved for poles. Today some couples spend a day in the woods looking for appropriate branches. And one couple fastened their *huppah* to brightly colored helium balloons!

The Huppah in the Ceremony. Stationary *huppot* are usually erected before the ceremony. If, however, the canopy is to be held by four honored guests, it can become part of

HUPPAH COVERS

the processional, with the pole bearers displaying the *huppah* as they walk down the aisle.

It is a special honor to be asked to hold a *huppah* pole. The four faces surrounding the couple represent the community that will help them establish a home.* In Orthodox communities it is still customary for all the guests—except the elderly and the ill—to remain standing throughout the ceremony to acknowledge the sanctity of the proceedings. However, since it's now customary for the company to sit, the *huppah* bearers act as representatives of the community in this regard as well.

Although most *huppot* are raised on the *bimah*, or platform, at one end of a synagogue or function room, some couples gather their guests around them in a circle or semicircle. In this way their new "home" is surrounded by the support and love of a community. This "*huppah*-in-the-round" arrangement also enables more guests to see the faces of the bride and groom.

There are many opinions and customs regarding who should and who should not stand under the *huppah* with the couple. Some believe that in order to ensure the validity of *nissuin*, only the bride and groom (not even the rabbi) should be covered by the canopy. Others feel that many family members and friends should stand with the couple to establish the tradition of *hachnasat orchim*—hospitality— in their home. Guests who participate in the ceremony— by reading a poem or chanting one of the wedding blessings —are often invited under the *huppah* when they address the couple.

A Family Heirloom. People who have spent time creating a *huppah* often display or use it again after the wedding. *Huppot* commonly appear as wall hangings in couples' bedrooms. Some suspend the canopy over their beds, recalling

---

* Since this is not a strictly religious duty, some rabbis suggest it as an appropriate way for non-Jewish friends to participate in the ceremony.

the original use of the *huppah* as a bridal chamber. Similarly, a *huppah* can be quilted and used as a bedcovering.

Homemade *huppot* are sometimes lent to special friends and family members for use in other weddings, and a few have been donated to synagogues for community use. But, generally, couples hold onto their *huppot* with hopes of seeing their children married under it. One couple raised their bridal canopy over their son's *bris* and their daughter's naming ceremony.

THE PROCESSIONAL

In the *shtetl* it was not uncommon for everyone who could walk to turn out to accompany the bride and groom to the synagogue. Israeli kibbutzniks have been ferried to their canopies on tractors, accompanied by virtually every man, woman, and child in the community. In America it is customary for rows of identically dressed young men and women to precede the bride's climactic entrance. These and other customs grew from the ancient practice of treating brides and grooms like royalty, deserving of a regal entourage. In Jewish tradition it is both an honor and an obligation to serve the wedding king and queen. Attending the bride was considered so important by the Talmudic rabbis that Rabbi Judah bar Il'ai is said to have instructed his students to put aside their studies to accompany a poor bride to her canopy.[23]

In American practice, fathers escort their daughters down the aisle to "give" them in marriage. The Jewish custom places far more emphasis on the role of both parents in leading their children—boys and girls—to marriage. A traditional Jewish processional is simplicity itself: the groom is brought to the canopy by his parents, the bride is brought by her parents, and the ceremony begins. In a common variation on this theme the two fathers escort the groom and the two mothers walk with the bride. Either arrangement demonstrates that marriage is a union of families, not just individuals, and acknowledges parents' dreams and efforts for their children's happiness. As there are no Halakhic rules on the composition and arrangement of processionals, most rabbis leave the matter up to the couple.

The roles of best man and maid/matron of honor have an ancient precedent in Judaism. Gabriel and Michael, two angels who attended the wedding of Adam and Eve, are considered the prototypical *shushvinim*—"friends"—of the bride and groom. Traditionally, the bride and groom have two *shushvinim* each, to act as their right and left hands. The groom's *shushvinim* may be put in charge of the ring(s), the bride may ask hers to hold the *ketubah* during the ceremony. The Yiddish name for these honored and important members of the wedding party, *unterfuhrers*, refers to the specific task of escorting the couple to the *huppah*. In some communities the *unterfuhrers* included two married couples —specifically, people who had been married only once. If brothers and sisters fell into this category, they would perform the honor. If not, other relatives or friends were asked.[24]

Processionals can easily be adapted to accommodate particular needs, such as the common but sometimes awkward situations created by divorce. Divorced and/or remarried parents may be uncomfortable at their childrens' weddings. The processional can be organized to include and honor them and minimize their discomfort.

If divorced parents of the bride and/or groom have an amicable relationship, there is no reason for them not to accompany their child down the aisle. Indeed, a child remains a living sign of a dream divorced parents once shared, a dream that certainly deserves to be remembered on this occasion.[25] If this arrangement causes any difficulty, each parent may be accompanied down the aisle by another of their children or by an escort. The bride or groom can then follow his/her parents unaccompanied. If the bride or groom have children from a previous marriage, they might be given roles to play in the processional, such as carrying the *ketubah* or the rings or acting as one of the *huppah* pole bearers.

Once the bride arrives at the *huppah*, it is customary for the groom to come out, meet her, and lead her into the *huppah*. This is a ritual enactment of the bride being taken into the groom's house. Sometimes the groom and bride will kiss their parents before entering the *huppah*. Couples who prefer to begin on a symbolically equal footing walk down the aisle together.

Here are a few options for ordering a processional:

TRADITIONAL/AMERICAN
> Rabbi and/or cantor and groom *(enter from a side entrance, without ceremony)*
> Bride's grandparents
> Groom's grandparents
> Usher,* bridesmaid
> Usher, bridesmaid
> Best man
> Groom's father, groom, groom's mother
> Usher, bridesmaid
> Usher, bridesmaid
> Maid of honor
> Bride's father, bride, bride's mother

SPECIAL CASE #1
> *Huppah* pole bearers
> Canopy bearers
> *Mesader kiddushin*
> Musicians

---

* In Orthodox settings, male and female escorts and attendants do not walk down the aisle together, and they remain separate throughout the ceremony and celebration.

Bride's daughter from a previous marriage carrying
flowers
Mother of groom with best man
Mother of bride with brother of bride
Father of bride with maid of honor
Groom and bride

INTIMATE/FAMILY
Grandparents of the bride
Grandfather of the groom with granddaughter
Groom's sister and brother
Groom's father, groom, groom's mother
Bride's sister
Bride's father, bride, bride's mother

SIMPLICITY REVISITED
Groom's attendants
Groom's parents
Groom
Bride's attendants
Bride's parents
Bride

There are no laws about who stands where beneath the
huppah. It is customary, however, for the bride to stand at
the groom's right. One of the most common arrangements
under the canopy looks like this:

	Rabbi		
Mother and	Groom	Bride	Mother and
father		Maid	father
of groom	Best man	of honor	of bride

Other attendants can be seated or remain standing around
the *huppah* in any order or pattern.

To avoid the need for and strain of a rehearsal, assign a
trusted relative or friend—someone who is not part of the

processional—to be in charge of it. Introduce him or her to everyone involved and write the order of the processional on a card. The "starter" collects and arranges the members of the party before their entrances and, on cue from the rabbi, sends them out in order and on time.

Music. The performance of music at a wedding is considered a religious obligation. In ancient times it was customary to play a flute before the bride and groom—a tradition some couples have reintroduced into the processional.

Processional music should be joyful but also purposeful and stately. (A livelier tune is usually reserved for the recessional.) It is customary for a single melody to accompany the entire processional, but if the bride is the last person to appear, one way to heighten the drama of her arrival is for the melody to change just before her entrance.

Something from the classical repertory is often played for wedding processionals, but many rabbis explicitly request that couples avoid the two most conventional selections—from Wagner's *Lohengrin* and Mendelssohn's *Midsummer Night's Dream*—pieces written by, respectively, a notorious anti-Semite and a Jew who converted to Christianity.

In the last century many American synagogues installed organs, which remain the musical standard in many communities. Although much Jewish music is not suited to the harmonic mode of the organ, simple, melodic arrangements can be quite beautiful. If you use the synagogue's organist, make an appointment to select music and musical styles, and if you have a favorite song you'd like played, find the sheet music and bring it to your meeting.

Israeli melodies, arranged for any combination of instruments and voices, make lovely processional accompaniments. Many of the most popular Hebrew songs for processionals are settings of poems from the Song of Songs, among them "Dodi li" (I Am My Beloved's), "Iti

Mil'Vanon" (Come With Me From Lebanon), and "Hanava Babanot" (Beautiful One). Other favorites include "Erev Shel Shoshanim" (Evening of Roses) and "Chorshat Hae-kalyptus" (The Eucalyptus Grove). Other sources for processional melodies include Yiddish folk songs and Sephardic music. To find sheet music and recordings of all sorts of wedding music, look in Jewish bookstores and in synagogue libraries. Many congregations don't require that you be a member to browse and copy.[26]

Any combination of instruments or voices can be effective accompaniment for the processional. Some common groupings are: guitar-recorder duet; string quartet; and flute, acoustic guitar, and cello. Orchestras and bands that play wedding receptions often include a flute player, who might be able and willing to provide the processional melody.

Another way of greeting the couple with music is for the guests to sing as the bride and groom walk to the *huppah*; Yemenite brides are sometimes preceded by a group of singing women. A trio or quartet of friends singing an Israeli love song in harmony can provide a very moving background. Or the rabbi, *mesader kiddushin*, or any designated song leader can, in a matter of minutes, teach all the guests a *niggun*, a wordless melody. No welcome to the *huppah* could be warmer or more personal than the singing of the people you love.

There is no good substitute for live music during the processional. A soloist playing virtually any instrument sets a mood (or, in biblical parlance, "gladdens the heart") as nothing else can. If, however, you decide to use a record or tape, it's a good idea to select something appropriate for the room's size—chamber music rather than a symphonic suite.

Candles. Light is a symbol of God's presence. The soft light of candles, which are associated with the joy of Shabbat and the holidays, can add a beautiful dimension to an evening ceremony. In some communities it is customary for those who lead the couple to the canopy to light the way with burning candles. In the past it was common for all the guests to carry candles—or torches—thus providing the light by which the ceremony was conducted. At the end of the ceremony these were tossed into the air along with the shouts of "Mazel tov!"

The beautiful braided candles of *havdalah* are often used for processionals, and these are now available in rainbows of color as well as the traditional blue and white. If, however, candles will be held by more than one or two members of the processional, it's probably wise to use dripless tapers and some sort of candle holders. Also, before proceeding with plans that include candles, make sure there are no problems with fire laws.

At one wedding each guest was handed a candle as she/he entered the sanctuary. The first two people in the processional acted as light bearers, row by row illuminating the candles of the people on the aisle, who in turn lit the candles of the people seated next to them, creating an ever-widening circle of light as the bride and groom walked into the room.

Some rabbis ask that the couple provide a pair of candlesticks under the *huppah*, which are meant to symbolize the beginning of a home that will be filled with the light of Shabbat and festival candles. When the bride and groom have arrived under the canopy, two attendants might light one candle each while someone reads this story from the Baal Shem Tov: "From every human being there rises a light that reaches straight to heaven. And when two souls that are destined for each other find one another, their streams of light flow together and a single brighter light goes forth from their united being."[27]

Circling. While there is a biblical source for the custom "A woman shall go around a man" (Jeremiah 31:22), the bride's circling the groom—either before entering the *hup-*

pah or sometime during the wedding ceremony—is not Halakhicly required. It is a very old custom that varies in practice; some circle three times, some seven times. Some brides are led around the groom by both mothers, and sometimes the entire processional circles him.

There are many explanations for the practice. Circling is a magical means of protection. By walking around the groom the bride creates an invisible wall to protect him from evil spirits, from the glances of other women, and from the temptations of the world. The bride's circle may also be seen as a way of binding the groom to her. Her circuits symbolically create a new family circle, demonstrating that her primary allegiance has shifted from her parents to her husband and that her husband is now bound to her more intimately than to his parents.[28]

Whether one performs three or seven circuits is a matter of family and community custom. Some have based their preference for three on the repetition in the Bible: "And I will betroth you to me forever. I will betroth you to me in righteousness, and in justice, and in loving-kindness, and in compassion; and I will betroth you to me in faithfulness" (Hosea 2:21-22). Also, a husband must fulfill three obligations to his wife: provide food and clothing and observe conjugal relations.

The mystical Cabalists preferred the number seven. Sevens abound in the Bible and throughout Jewish life. The world was created in seven days, and marriage is a seven-days-a-week act of creation. With marriage, seven of the bride's relatives are forbidden to the groom.[29] There are seven wedding blessings. And circling is thought of as the way the bride enters the groom's *s'ferot*—the mystical spheres of his soul that correspond to the seven lower attributes of God.

In the past few generations liberal Jews have abandoned the custom because of its magical connotations and because of the apparent subservience in the bride's circuits around her "master." Recently, however, some couples have reclaimed this custom with both new interpretations and new ritual forms. Some women have reintroduced the bride's circling, seeing it not as a token of subservience but as a powerful act of definition: she creates the space the couple will share.

Many couples prefer to mutualize this gesture. At some weddings the bride circles the groom clockwise (three or seven times), and then the groom repeats the gesture counterclockwise around the bride, or bride and groom hold hands and walk in a circle, ring-around-the-rosie style. Either way, the double circling physically demonstrates independent and complementary orbits. This kind of circling has been accompanied by strains of music or with the words of a poem or prayer found or written for the occasion. This is another place that Shir haShirim, the Song of Songs, is especially appropriate.

One couple completely redefined the meaning of circling and composed a chant that was sung by their guests:

> *Circle round for freedom*
> *Circle round for peace*
> *For all of us imprisoned*
> *Circle for release.*
>
> *Circle for the planet*
> *Circle for each soul*
> *For the future of our unborn*
> *Keep the Circle whole.*[30]

The Recessional. After the glass is broken the bride and groom leave the *huppah* to the sounds of joyous, up-tempo music. One of the most popular selections for this is the Israeli song "Od Yishama" (Again Will Be Heard). Other common songs are "Siman Tov u'Mazel Tov" (A Good Sign and Good Luck) and "Yasis Alayich" (May God Rejoice) or any upbeat song.[31]

The notion of a formal recessional developed at least in part to facilitate the receiving line. After the bride and groom make their exit, the parents of the couple walk back up the aisle, followed by the rabbi, grandparents, and attendants. Generally, members of the processional leave in the reverse order of their arrival.

If the couple is going to *yichud*, however, there is no receiving line and therefore less need for a recessional. Once the bride and groom leave, the parents of the couple embrace and guests surround them with congratulations. If the celebration is to be held at the same location, hors d'oeuvres and champagne are served immediately. At high-spirited weddings the music that greets the breaking of the glass is the signal for dancing to begin. In some cases guests will dance, accompanying the bride and groom to *yichud*.

At one wedding, after the bride and groom had departed for *yichud*, the rabbi—who had earlier described the special, spiritually charged nature of the space beneath the *huppah*—invited everyone who wished to to stand beneath the canopy for a few moments.

The Receiving-Line Dilemma. Yichud means never having to stand on a receiving line—a welcome excuse for people who dread the drawn-out repetitive ritual of meeting and greeting that is still standard practice at most American weddings.

Receiving lines do, however, fulfill important functions. For one thing, they give parents a chance to *kvell*—to bask in their children's happiness. Also, a formal line means the couple has the opportunity to at least say hello to all their guests, something that might not otherwise happen. It means everyone gets the chance to meet all the principals and allows people to match names and faces. "So *you're* Cousin Susan!" "So *you're* the friend who flew in from Israel!" "So you're Myra's mother!"

Receiving lines are also something of an ordeal, especially at a wedding of any size. For the guests the waiting is always a little awkward, and then there's never enough time to say more than a quick "Mazel tov." After a while the receivers are bound to get tired (not to mention hungry), and their greetings and smiles begin to feel wooden.

When *yichud* is observed, many couples simply forgo the receiving line and allow guests to seek them out for a private moment during the celebration. Of course, the couple's families can still create a receiving line to accept congratulations and *kvell*. (If this is your plan, and your parents will be meeting many of your friends for the first time, it's helpful to get an attendant to stand in line and help with introductions.) Some couples have come up with alternatives to the receiving line that ensure them the chance to share a word with all their guests during the *simcha*. These are described in the following chapters.

WITNESSES

A marriage can be valid without a rabbi but not without witnesses. Since witnessing is considered a great responsibility, the bride and groom select witnesses they trust and respect. Because they are so important in "making" the marriage, it has been suggested that witnesses assume a responsibility that lasts "for one hundred and twenty years"—the number of years given to Moses.

The Hebrew word for "witness," *ayd*, shares a common root with the word *od*, meaning "duration"; a witness gives permanence to human activities that are transitory. [32] While a room filled with people might see a wedding take place, only the designated witnesses have the power to validate the subtle transaction at the core of the ceremony.* The

---

* Some authorities claim that the two people who witness the *ketubah* should not be the same ones who witness the wedding. This opinion provides another opportunity to involve and honor a few more special friends in the ceremony. However, there is disagreement on this point, and in many cases the same people witness both *ketubah* and ceremony.

rabbis understood that family members might have more of an emotional, social, or even economic stake in what transpired under the *huppah*, which is why *unrelated* observers are specified.

Because they play such a vital role, there have always been strict and specific laws about who is a kosher witness. According to Halakhah, witnesses must be observant Jewish men over the age of thirteen who are unrelated to each other or to the bride or groom. If these conditions are not met, the marriage is legally suspect, which is why it became customary for the officiating cantor and rabbi to serve as witnesses.

The Halakhic "exemption" of women from participation in communal worship and public events is usually attributed to the Talmud's respect for their special duties in the home. While many Jews no longer recognize the validity of this ruling, and it is common for women to act as witnesses at Reform weddings, those who wish to fulfill the letter of the law but also want to affirm the presence and participation of women sometimes name two Jewish men and two Jewish women as their witnesses.

Criteria for what constitutes an observant Jew obviously invite disagreement. In some circles observance is equated with the title *shomer shabbos*, someone who obeys the commandments regarding Shabbat, who also obeys the laws of *kashrut*, and is mindful of the Torah's moral commandments. Of course a Jew considered "observant" by one group of people might be considered a heretic by another, but it is considered a sin to embarrass anyone with inquisitions into his or her personal habits and religious practice. According to the rabbinic adage, "One who shames his neighbor has no share in the world to come."[33]

Non-Jews are not permitted to act as witnesses because they are not bound to the religious and legal system that sanctions a Jewish marriage. Few rabbis will accept non-Jewish witnesses, although those who do not abide by other Halakhic rules (regarding gender, for instance) may admit a non-Jew who is informed of the duties and obligations entailed by this honor.

At the *ketubah* signing or before the ceremony begins, the rabbi may introduce the witnesses and explain their responsibilities. Sometimes witnesses are questioned to make sure they are qualified and understand their role and to determine whether they are willing to stand by the couple through the challenges and difficulties of their marriage.

The witnesses are assigned a position where they can see and hear the bride and groom. The bride and groom must also be able to see the witnesses and be aware of their identity and role. In traditional ceremonies the rabbi asks that the witnesses examine the ring and testify that it is worth one *prutah*, the smallest coin used in ancient times, before the groom gives it to the bride. The witnesses must see him put the ring on her finger and hear his recitation of the marriage formula: *"Harey aht me'kudeshet li. . ."* (With this ring you are consecrated to me . . .). Although the bride is not required to say anything in response, the witnesses must see that she willingly consents to the marriage.

Witnesses are sometimes asked to attest to the validity of the couple's *yichud* as well. They watch the bride and groom enter a room they have determined to be empty, stand guard over the couple's privacy, and finally, watch as wife and husband emerge.

A JEWISH CHECKLIST

Weddings breed lists at an alarming rate, but it's a good idea to have one special list for ceremonial items. On the day of the wedding it should be entrusted to a reliable person who will make sure everything is ready and in place:

- Table(s) and tablecloths (for *ketubah* signing, and under the *huppah*)

- *Ketubah*, and pen (with correct color of ink!)
- *Huppah* and poles
- *Kiddush* cups and wine
- Glass for breaking (in a napkin or pouch)
- Ring(s)
- Candles and matches
- Wedding booklets
- *Kippot* (yarmulkes) for guests
- Signs that direct guests to groom's table and bride's room
- Et cetera

PLANNING
THE PARTY

FOOD AND DRINK

Making It a Simcha. The meal that follows a Jewish wedding is a *s'eudah mitzvah,* a meal to accompany the fulfillment of a religious commandment.*According to tradition, any communal meal can be consecrated if it includes some religious content, some "words of Torah." Hasidim consider the table an altar where words and songs are offerings to God. According to *Pirke Avot* (Words of the Fathers), ". . . if three have eaten at a table and have spoken words of Torah, it is as if they have eaten from the table of God." At a wedding, everything that increases happiness praises God: words of Torah, blessings, songs, dances, toasts, reminiscences, and jokes that make the bride and groom laugh.

"Reception" is not the right word for what happens after the *huppah; simcha* is more accurate. *Simcha* means "joy" as well as the "celebration of a joyous event," and the purpose of Jewish wedding parties is to increase the happiness of the bride and groom. The Talmud says that someone who

* In addition to weddings, *s'eudot mitzvah* follow major life-cycle events, including circumcision, bar or bat mitzvah, the completion of a course of Jewish study, and funerals.

enjoys a wedding feast but does nothing to rejoice the hearts of the bride and groom has transgressed against the "five voices": the voice of joy, the voice of gladness, the voice of the bridegroom, the voice of the bride, and the voice that praises God. This section offers ideas and strategies for fulfilling the holiest, happiest goal of the wedding celebration—increasing the *simcha* of bride and groom.

Kashrut. Planning the menu for a *s'eudah mitzvah* requires giving some thought to *kashrut*—the system of laws that govern what and how Jews eat. By following *kashrut* you avoid discomfort—and hunger—for observant relatives and friends.* Indeed, your rabbi may not be able to enjoy (or even feel able to attend) your *simcha* if the food is non-kosher. Providing a meal that conforms to the fundamentals of *kashrut* announces your intention to honor Jewish law, even if you don't plan to establish a kosher kitchen in your home.

Kashrut is best understood not as an ancient means of preserving human health but as a way of sanctifying a basic need. "Israel is commanded to hallow the act of eating and through this making holy, become holy."[34] It is based on specific proscriptions in the Bible—for example, those against eating birds of prey and bottom-feeding fish. The separation of dairy and meat products is an elaboration on the Torah's command not to "boil a kid in its mother's milk."

In a nutshell, *kashrut* permits the following foods to be eaten: all vegetables and fruits, fish with fins and scales (no shellfish), domestic fowl, and animals that both chew their cud and have split hooves. For meat to be kosher, however, the animal must be killed according to specific ritual laws by someone who recites a blessing and then soaked and salted to remove any trace of blood. Finally, meat and milk

---

* Of course, levels of observance vary tremendously, and even an Orthodox-approved catering service may not satisfy a Szatmár uncle.

products are not eaten at the same meal and must be kept separate. To fully observe this injunction, *milchig* (dairy) and *flayshig* (meat) foods are not cooked in the same pots or served on the same dishes. The customary waiting period between consumption of meat and milk varies from one to six hours.[35]

Synagogues require that food be prepared and served in accordance with the dietary laws. Many congregations provide couples with a guidebook for use in their kitchens, and some allow only selected kosher caterers to work in their kitchens. Your rabbi should be able to direct you to local kosher caterers, and the Yellow Pages of most large towns and cities often have a special listing of kosher services under "Catering." Jewish newspapers and kosher meat markets and grocery stores might also provide names of smaller catering services. "Kosher style" denotes Jewish-identified foods such as lox and knishes, but it is generally a signal that *kashrut* is not observed.

Given the recent trend toward leaner diets and the fact that most families now include some vegetarians, a dairy meal that features fish (which is *pareve*—neither milk nor meat) is often the simplest solution to a whole range of dietary requirements. In the past, caterers did their best to dissuade people from this kind of meal, in large part because meat entrées are much more profitable. But now that salmon has become a fashionable (and profitable) main course, it is easier to get caterers to provide a full-course *milchig* meal.

Coping with Caterers. A wise rabbi once conferred the title "Levites" upon all caterers.[36] While members of this tribe were not priests (Kohanim) but assistants to priests, they performed indispensable and holy duties in the Temple. But when Levites begin to act like Kohanim—if your caterer obscures the simple truth that it is her function to make things easy for you and not vice versa—there's bound to be trouble.

The food at a wedding celebration should add to the pleasure of the bride and groom. If you hate prime ribs, for heaven's sake don't order them—even if the caterer insists they're his specialty and your guests will be expecting them. Ask questions. Negotiate. Shop around. Even if your choices are limited because you're looking for a kosher caterer in a small city, the same criteria apply to all Levites, everywhere.

In general, the larger the caterer, the less personal the service and the more institutional the food. The same usually holds true for hotels, where food is prepared in quantity. Meals served by large operations are invariably passable but rarely memorable. However, only large firms are able to accommodate weddings of more than two hundred or two hundred fifty. Caterers for big crowds will provide everything from liquor to a master of ceremonies and musicians. For weddings of two hundred people or fewer, most communities have a good selection of fine small-to-medium-sized catering companies from which to choose.

The best way to find a good caterer is by word of mouth. Ask everyone you know—from the rabbi to colleagues at work—for suggestions. If you're browsing through the Yellow Pages, pay attention to the smaller ads and single-line entries with interesting names. Many of these will consist of a talented cook (or two) who prepares food in her own kitchen. Small but elegant caterers often advertise in the back pages of city magazines. There are increasing numbers of kosher caterers of this sort—women who take great pride in serving beautiful, gourmet food that conforms to the dietary laws. Keep your eyes open for specialty shops that sell homemade salads, soups, breads, and desserts; many of these retail businesses also run catering services. Also, many restaurants will serve special meals in their dining room, in your rented hall, or in a private home. Vegetarian restaurants are a good source for *milchig* meals.

Before calling a caterer be ready with the following information: the date and time of your wedding, an approximate number of guests, location, and cooking facilities. (You can't expect anyone to provide a full-course dinner for eighty in a closet-sized kitchen.) And be prepared to give the caterer some idea of your budget. (It's not a great idea to look for bargains, however; if the price is too good to be true, the food isn't going to be.) With this information, the caterer should be able to determine whether he's able to and interested in doing your wedding.

If the person on the other end of the line is curt, impatient, or in any way unpleasant, call another caterer. Graciousness is an important part of serving a meal, and your initial contact is a pretty good indicator of what you can expect from further dealings. You're going to be working closely with this person, so if you feel any discomfort, look for someone else. When you find someone who is willing and able to take on your wedding—someone you like— make an appointment to meet. Some caterers will charge a fee for an initial consultation, but many will talk with you free of charge.

Before your meeting, make notes about what you would and would not like to have served. Some caterers show sample menus and even photographs of their work, but it is most important to get a list of recent clients as references. Any reputable caterer will be happy to provide you with some. (When you call for references, make sure to ask about the quantity as well as the quality of the food.) In some cases you might even arrange to discreetly watch a caterer in action—but don't expect free samples.

Most caterers charge on a per-person basis, even for buffet meals. When estimating the guest list, consider whether you intend to feed the musicians and/or photographer, since you will be charged for them. A last-minute guest or two extra rarely presents a problem, but if twenty "extras" arrive at the buffet table, you risk not having enough food, and the caterer will legitimately charge for them.

Caterers usually ask for a deposit of 30 to 50 percent of

their estimate, with the balance due on the day of the wedding. Many states have a meal tax that is added to the bill. No matter whom you choose as a caterer, it is essential to have a written contract that spells out your agreement. This doesn't have to be an elaborate document; it can be a simple letter or memo that itemizes the particulars, including date, menu, and an estimate of the price.

The caterer's price may include any and all of the following: rental of linen, china, silverware, and liquor; the wedding cake, waiters and bartenders, and, in some cases, even musicians. The larger the caterer, the more is (or can be) included in his price. If the caterer provides a full bar, for example, you'll be paying for the time he spends ordering the liquor as well as for the beverages, plus some markup.

Wedding consultants, or "accommodators," are contractors who can be hired to do all the planning. They will rent the hall, tables, chairs, linens, dishes, and glassware; find and hire the caterer, band, and clean-up crew; even tend to the printing of the invitations and newspaper announcements. Many—though by no means all—of these services are high-powered, expensive, and tend to err on the *Goodbye, Columbus* side of things. Again, the best way to find an accommodator is by word of mouth.

The Semicatered and the Potluck Wedding. Any involvement of wedding guests is a *mitzvah* for them and for the bride and groom. If your wedding is informal and/or you want to minimize expenses, a caterer can be hired as an "expediter" rather than the sole provisioner. Professional supervision over a carefully orchestrated potluck meal can result in quite an elegant repast.

Since the presentation of food is very important, a caterer can be brought in to help lay out a buffet—to decorate platters and arrange the food so that it is accessible as well as attractive. Or he could prepare parts of the meal—hot hors d'oeuvres and the main course, for example—while guests bring salads and sweets. Rather than have a dozen random salads, he might even suggest three or four easy ones that a number of people would be asked to make at home and deliver before the ceremony begins.

Many caterers are not interested in this kind of work because of its low profit margin. But small, young businesses are often glad to oblige. Or a caterer might agree to act as a "consultant" and recommend some of her assistants to work in the kitchen and as servers on the wedding day.

Potluck buffets full of favorite family recipes and friends' specialties add a kind of *haimishness*—homeyness—to the party. Some couples include a note with the invitation asking guests to bring a covered dish to the party. In order to avoid an all-dessert or all-salad meal, specify what kind of dish should be brought, the quantity desired, and of course any dietary requirements (that is, *milchig*, or vegetarian, or *flayshig*).

Wedding Cakes. Weddings mean cakes. For some people it's not a *real* wedding without a four-foot-tall, three-tiered white cake with bride and groom statuettes on the top. For others it's not a wedding without a piece of *laykach*—sponge cake—with a glass of Manischewitz sweet blackberry wine to wash it down.

The wedding cakes baked in most commercial bakeries consist largely of powdered sugar and vegetable shortening and taste accordingly. There are, however, pastry chefs (and bakeries) that specialize in large cakes made with the finest ingredients. Some caterers make wonderful, rich cakes, and anyone who caters weddings should be able to recommend a good bakery or an individual who bakes in her own kitchen. Wedding cakes are quite expensive, with prices calculated by the slice, but it rarely costs more to buy a fine cake than one made primarily of powdered sugar and Crisco.

It's become quite common for friends to make wedding cakes as gifts. Many kitchen-supply stores carry large pans and cake-decorating equipment and instruction books. Virtually any good-sized cake adorned with fresh flowers can become a wedding cake.

Le'chaim. The Hasidim have long considered drink a legitimate tool for creating *simcha.* The open bar has recently become a common feature at Jewish weddings, finally disproving (for better or worse) the truism "Jews don't drink." But the bar, like the menu, can reflect your tastes and preferences. Champagne alone or wine and beer in abundance can certainly suffice. And there should always be plenty of nonalcoholic beverages as well.

As far as *kashrut*'s application to potables is concerned, the Torah prohibits Jews from drinking any wine that has been used in connection with idolatry. The Talmud later extended this prohibition to all wines produced by non-Jews, although the restriction never applied to wine made from fruit other than grapes or to grain liquors. Virtually all Reform and many Conservative synagogues allow wine that is not designated "kosher." Some couples make a point of serving Israeli wine, both to support Israel and as a sign of Jewish identification.

If you're having more than eighty guests or so, even at a semicatered or potluck *simcha,* it's a good idea to have someone tending bar—if only to open wine and soda bottles and make sure there is enough ice. The caterer may hire a bartender or you can ask friends to do the honors, but since this can be a full-time job, volunteers should be assigned short stints so they can also join the party.

LAUGHTER, MUSIC, AND DANCE

Reinventing the Badchan. Spontaneous observance of the ancient injunction to "rejoice the bride and groom" usually requires some careful groundwork. This need not (and should not) involve much time or effort from bride or

Kiddush Cup

Cups and plate: © Leslie Gattmann and Eugene Frank
Photos: Peggy McMahon

Commemorative Plate

groom—a little delegating of responsibility and some explicit hinting should suffice.

One couple simply penned a note on the map to their synagogue that said: "Jewish tradition treats the bride and groom as king and queen. The main purpose of the wedding party is to entertain the couple. In this spirit we hope you'll come prepared with a story, a poem, a joke to tell, a song to sing—maybe even a magic trick—along with your best dancing shoes and a happy heart." The results of this extra invitation hint included everything from beautiful poems to shaggy-dog stories, from an eight-year-old's violin debut to folk songs by two semiprofessional grown-up performers—even a couple of magic tricks!

These entertainments were presented during the wedding feast and punctuated the performance of a master of ceremonies *par excellence*, a close friend who had long harbored a secret ambition to be a stand-up comedian. His monologue included sight gags and toasts, the story of how the bride and groom met, and elaborate introductions for every "act." He announced the start of the dancing, he informed the company when dessert was served. Most important, he set a joyful example.

In other words, he acted as a modern-day *badchan*—literally, "joker." Also called *leytzan*—clown—and *marshalik* —marshal—the *badchan* was an indispensable part of Eastern European weddings for nearly seven centuries. The word *badchan* comes from a Talmudic verb that means "to cheer up" or "to make laugh." He was a paid professional, a combination jester, preacher, singer, rhymester, and toastmaster. He could be crude and earthy (he even announced the size of cash gifts), but he was also supposed to be a learned man whose witticisms were based in biblical verses and passages of Talmud. He told anecdotes about the guests, he posed riddles, he dispensed compliments; in other words, he could really make or break a *simcha*.[38]

An accomplished *badchan* could elicit tears as well as laughter. One of his most important duties was presiding

at the *bedeken*, at which he was expected to make a sentimental speech to the bride about the cruel passage of time.
But the *badchan*'s primary function was to make people
laugh. Like all good comedians, he made light of current
tensions—and when any two families marry each other,
tensions abound. The *badchan* has been credited with keeping Jewish humor alive even during some of Eastern European Jewry's darkest hours. Indeed, the flowering of
Yiddish theater and literature in the nineteenth and early
twentieth centuries probably owes a great deal to the per-
sistence of *badchanut*—the art of the *badchan*.

It is not difficult to reinvent the *badchan* for modern pur-
poses. All that is needed is a willing friend or member of
the family, someone who knows how to tell a joke, who is
willing to share the microphone, who is not afraid to make
a fool of him- or herself. Once the bride and groom entrust
someone with the job, the *badchan* should be allowed free
reign and should be given background information on both
families to use as material for monologues; the more personal the *badchan*'s anecdotes and jokes, the better.

The *badchan* may also have more serious emcee responsibilities, such as making the first toast, announcing dinner,
reading telegrams from absent friends or family members,
introducing the band, and leading the company in the
blessings after the meal. As with *badchanut* of old, senti-
ment plays an indispensable role. The master of ceremonies
can give people permission to put their feelings into words,
with toasts offered as blessings. She/he may invite the
learned guests to give a *vort* or *d'var Torah*—some thoughts
about the week's Torah portion. Guests may compose
original poems and songs to honor the bride and groom;
others might want to read a favorite quotation or poem as a
gift.

The *badchan*'s main task is to orchestrate the entertain-
ment, to which end she/he may wish to line up some speakers and performers or even instigate some *mishegas*
(foolishness) in advance of the wedding.

• One *badchan* began by "crowning" the couple with foil-covered crowns and scepters and leading them to a pair of elaborately decorated "thrones," which were wheeled in by a few costumed coconspirators, who then proceeded to juggle—very badly and very funnily.

• Song parodies (set to any popular tune) about the bride and groom are common, and lyrics can even be printed and distributed to all the guests for a comic serenade. For a sing-along in Hebrew and/or Yiddish, transliterated versions help ensure full participation.

• Other forms of modern *badchanut* have included card tricks, acrobatics, and vaudeville routines. At one wedding a dramatization of the couple's first date was performed by two of the youngest children present. In preparation for another wedding, some enterprising friends got the bride and groom to pose for pictures, which they then developed into a kind of "This Is Your Life" slide show. One *badchan*, a gifted improviser, distributed cards and asked guests to return them with questions they'd always wanted to ask about Jewish weddings—and answered them all with outrageous lies.

Historically, Jewish wedding celebrations have reflected the state of the arts of the culture and time. During the Italian Renaissance, guests composed sonnets and performed elaborate pageants and plays as grand and as elegant as anything the secular culture had to offer. At Yemenite weddings, professional singers and dancers are sometimes hired to perform. Today an original videotape could be part of the *simcha*, or tape-recorded messages from guests who were unable to attend the party could be played, or a bouquet of balloons could be presented or released.

Music. There is a Hasidic saying, "When two who cannot sing raise their voices together, a miracle happens." Anything from sentimental ballads to silly parodies to folk tunes to camp songs can turn a group of strangers into a community. Song sheets and a willing song leader can help unite the guests into an unforgettable serenade for the bride and groom. (Guitars are helpful in this but not crucial.)

There is no Halakhic ruling against hiring a string quartet to provide stately classical music while your guests mingle and eat. However, since dancing is a traditional and treasured feature of Jewish weddings (see below), dance bands are generally preferred.

Groups that play at weddings vary in quality, but most have a familiar repertoire consisting mostly of "standards": big-band classics and show tunes, a couple of rock-and-roll songs ("for the young people"), and the usual list of ethnic melodies—for Jewish weddings these usually include "Hava Nagila" for a hora and a medley from *Fiddler on the Roof*. Some bandleaders expect to act as master of ceremonies throughout a wedding party, announcing the meal, the cake cutting, the bouquet tossing. Bands that work closely with caterers have a tendency to be more attuned to the needs of the kitchen than to the fact that the dance floor is packed and you'd rather wait dessert for fifteen minutes. Whomever you hire, make sure the leader understands what you do and don't expect of him. If you don't want to hear "Sunrise, Sunset," make that clear. If a *badchan* will be running the show, inform the bandleader that you expect him to take his cues from your master of ceremonies. Even if there's no *badchan*, appoint an ambassador to the bandleader to let your wishes be known. And, of course, never hire a band without a hearing; if a live audition is impossible, at least get hold of a tape.

The revival of *klezmer* music has reintroduced an old option to Jewish wedding music. *Klezmer*, a term that refers to both the music and the musicians, was once so traditional at Eastern European weddings that the phrase "a wedding without *klezmorim*" described any lifeless, colorless event.[39] The music is a wild mishmash of influences: military marches, melodies by the great masters, folk songs, and dance tunes. When *klezmer* came to America, new instruments were added and jazz licks crept in. Although *klezmer* bands never died out altogether, most American Jews dismissed *klezmer* as embarrassingly old-country—unsophisticated and overly sentimental "green-horn" trash.

In the past decade accomplished young Jewish musicians have researched the Old World standards, dug up early recordings, and begun performing and releasing new records. *Klezmer* ensembles (which now include vocalists and instruments ranging from tubas to accordions) are currently in demand for non-Orthodox weddings. Even a small *klezmer* group can be very effective; one clarinet, a piano (or accordion), and a bass can get everyone up and dancing. Most of the new *klezmer* groups are based in major cities—New York, Boston, Chicago, San Francisco. Your rabbi or cantor should be able to tell you if there are any *klezmorim* nearby and help you get in touch with them.

Even if you can't find a *klezmer* band in your community, or if you want more variety in the music at your wedding, there are ways to include this music's sound and spirit. Some wedding bands are very accommodating, and if you give the bandleader a *klezmer* record and some sheet music, he may be willing to rehearse and play a few numbers.* An even simpler alternative is to play a *klezmer* record or tape while the band is taking a break. Although it can't match the excitement of a live performance, a full program of taped music is an inexpensive alternative to hiring musicians. And recordings obviously allow you to please the broadest range of musical tastes.

Dancing. The Talmud asks, "How should one dance before the bride?" Judah bar Ilai answered by dancing with a myrtle twig. Rabbi Aha danced with the bride on his shoul-

---

* Recordings, sheet music, and songbooks are sold at many Jewish bookstores. Many city and college libraries have large collections of Jewish music, as do some synagogues. Local cantors can be good resources, and, of course, all the Jewish seminaries have impressive collections of sheet music and records.[40]

ders. Even as a very old man, Samuel bar Rav Isaac would perform his wedding specialty—juggling three myrtle twigs while he danced and sang. At his funeral a heavenly flame burned above his coffin, as God's token of appreciation for those pious performances.[41]

Jewish wedding dances are probably as old as Jewish weddings. In the Song of Songs there is mention of a "dance of two companies." Even after the rabbis grew suspicious of celebrations that threw men and women into each other's arms, dancing remained a cherished feature of wedding celebrations. While "ballroom" remains the most common form of music and dancing at American weddings, the development of Israeli folk dancing and the *klezmer* revival have begun to challenge the stately fox trot and waltz.

Dancing to *klezmer* and Israeli folk music tends to involve groups of people rather than couples. The steps can be as simple as walking or skipping in time to the music, so all that's required are some infectious tunes and a core of enthusiasts. The *badchan* or someone else can act as "dance master," announcing: "This *freilach* [happy song] is for men only" or "All couples who have been married for less than five years up next; women line up on this side, the men on that side, clapping hands, walk to the middle of the room," and so on. This kind of dancing sweeps nearly everyone onto the dance floor—even people who insist they can't dance at all.

Israeli dancing ranges from simple circle dances to elaborate duets. Friends who are accomplished dancers might perform some of the more complex steps—especially those set to lyrics from *Shir haShirim* (Song of Songs)—and teach some more simple dances.

In eastern European tradition, one of the first dances is usually some version of the *Mitzvah Tanz*, the dance of the commandment. Since dancing with the bride is a *mitzvah*, and since every *mitzvah* deserves individual celebration, it became customary for everyone to have a turn with the bride. The fathers usually went first, then the bridegroom, and scholars and important members of the community next. This *mitzvah* was so important that brides would invite beggars to dance with them as an act of *tsedakah* (charity).

Modern versions of the *Mitzvah Tanz* include women as well as men, all of whom try to dance for at least a moment with both the bride and groom. Sometimes this begins with the groom asking his mother to dance, and then the bride's mother. Meanwhile the bride dances with her father, and then her husband's father. Next, all the women circle the bride, and all the men circle the groom, and each dancer enters the middle to take a quick turn with the wedding queen or king.

Perhaps the best known of all Jewish wedding-dance customs is the moment at which the bride and groom are raised on the shoulders of their guests—usually in chairs. This happens at the height of the festivities, or whenever the melody and mood is right. Sometimes the couple will be whirled around each other, holding the ends of a handkerchief, sometimes the couple is paraded around the room in a processional. One theory for the origin of this custom is that during the days when bride and groom were separated by a *mechitzah*—a physical barrier between the sexes—the added height let them catch a glimpse of each other. But the custom probably has as much to do with the privileges of royalty, who have been carried in chairs and on litters from earliest times.

There are dozens of *tanzen*, dances associated with weddings. The following are some of the simple combinations and story dances that can be announced and improvised:

- The *Machetunim Tanz* gets the newly related families out on the dance floor together.
- The *Bobbes Tanz* is reserved for grandmothers only.
- In the *Broiges Tanz* a man and woman pantomime a quarrel and reconciliation.

• In the *Huppah Tanz* friends whirl around the bride and groom holding a *tallis* or a tablecloth over their heads.

• In the *Besem Tanz* a broom is a prop used as a horse, a yoke, a musical instrument, or anything else that occurs to the dancer. In pantomime dances like this one, it's common to act out the stages of a marriage: courting, *huppah*, work, children, old age.

• The *Flash Tanz* requires some skill and rehearsal since it involves balancing a bottle on the forehead or on top of the head while moving to the music.

• There are countless kinds of *Freilachs*—happy songs —and these inspire all kinds of horseplay, from tying napkins together for a session of jump-rope to a full-fledged Jewish square dance, complete with alle-mandes. Cossack dances such as the *Kazatsky* feature strenuous deep-knee-bend kicks and often lead to con-tests of skill, strength, and endurance.

• The song "Keytzed M'Rakdim Lifnei Hakallah" (How Should One Dance Before the Bride?) is often performed in lines facing the bride and groom. Groups of women and men walk toward the couple and meet in the center of the dance floor for curtsies, bows, and other movements.

• The *Mizinke*, usually performed to the Yiddish song "Die Mezinke Oysgegeben" (The Youngest Daughter Is Given) is one of the last dances. This is a tribute to a mother who has brought her last daughter to the canopy. Today the custom is commonly extended to both father and mother to commemorate their last child's *huppah*—son or daughter. Seated on chairs in the center of the dance floor, the parents are presented with bouquets and circled by the company in a dance that celebrates the completion of their parental respon-sibility. A variation of this theme is the *Krenzl*, or crowning (usually with a wreath of flowers) of the mother (or mothers) who has just seen her last child wed. "Die Mizinke Oysgegeben" is anything but a sad song. One of the lyrics asks, "Isaac, you rascal, why is your bow silent? Are the musicians playing or sleeping? Have them tear the strings apart. My youngest daughter is getting married!"

Of course, not all the dancing has to be "Jewish." Any music—from big-band tunes to current pop songs—that gets people up and rejoicing is a *mitzvah*. Indeed, many eastern European and Israeli dances are based on the local steps of neighboring communities. The hora, for example, perhaps the best known of all Israeli dances, is not a product of the Middle East at all but a Romanian folk dance!

PHOTOGRAPHERS AND FLOWERS

Weddings are for rejoicing, not posing. But you can never have too many pictures of your own wedding. Dilemma: What's a couple to do?

The wedding photographer has become something of a notorious character—an authoritarian figure whose pictures are entirely predictable. Actually, predictability is a major selling point of the "packages" offered by photography studios. Most people want the standard pictures of the principals: bride, groom, their families and attendants—and for good reason. These photos take their place in a gallery of family portraits, and even the corniest poses—like cutting the wedding cake—assume historical proportions when placed next to a nearly identical shot of your parents doing precisely the same thing thirty-five years ago.

One of the problems with this kind of wedding photography is that it sometimes misses the day's spirit. Studio or formal wedding photographers often have a rigid idea of how and when and why things get done. The result is usually a series of high-quality eight-by-ten color glossies, delivered already arranged and bound. The pictures tend to be entirely posed, with "action" shots limited to cake cutting and bouquet tossing. Most studios, of course, will include as many additional pictures as you are willing to pay for. So if you have particular action shots in mind— pictures of the dancing, for example—arrange to speak well in advance to the person assigned to shoot your wedding.

There are always snapshot takers at weddings to supplement the professional's work.* The presence of a few serious amateur photographers can help document the festivities—from the groom's table to your three-year-old niece wearing salad all over her best dress—leaving the portraits to the pros. Remember that asking a friend to act as "official" photographer may well put a crimp in his or her enjoyment of the party.

Seeking an alternative to the formal wedding photographer, some couples employ professionals who work with 35-millimeter cameras, using a more editorial, candid approach to the event, which results in a less formal but more nearly complete record of the day. You don't buy a "package" of pictures from informal photographers so much as their skill and sensitivity. While the cost is not necessarily less than that for a studio photographer, the 35-millimeter option yields many more pictures from which to choose.

Photographers who take informal wedding pictures get most of their assignments from word-of-mouth recommendations and are rarely listed in the Yellow Pages as wedding photographers. Ask your rabbi for a referral or for the names of couples who employed informal photographers at their weddings. Sometimes caterers and florists can be of help. Once you've found some candidates, make appointments to see their portfolios. In addition to printed pictures, ask to see contact sheets of weddings they've shot to give you an idea of their over-all approach.

Whomever you hire, give your photographer a schedule of the events you want her to shoot and also a list of people

* Some photographers do not permit anyone else to operate a camera while they're on duty, so check this with whomever you hire!

you especially want photos of. (Pictures of the immediate family may be obvious, but what about your favorite but shy Aunt Ruth or your friend who flew in from Argentina just for the wedding?) The more thorough your list, the better. Even if she is familiar with Jewish weddings, tell the photographer about the particulars of yours. Do you want her at the *ketubah* signing and the veiling? Do you want pictures of the wedding *challah* and the blessing before the meal? Do you want her to concentrate on the dancing or is it more important to get a clear shot of every table?

Formal group portraits are best taken immediately after the ceremony or directly following *yichud*. Wedding photographers are skilled at organizing and expediting these sessions, which are invariably rushed, since guests are waiting for the bride and groom to appear. To speed things along, the photographer might take some group portraits earlier: the groom with his parents outside the synagogue, the bride with her parents at the veiling. It is disruptive (and sometimes impossible) to collect everyone for formal portraits later, although less formal group shots—four aunts sitting at one table, a group of cousins gathered at the bar—can be taken throughout the festivities.

Most rabbis do not allow flash photography during the ceremony. (Because video cameras are less intrusive, some will allow filming.) Generally, this means pictures of the processional are fine, and once the glass is shattered, the shutters may fly again, but the proceedings under the *huppah* are off limits. In any event, check with your rabbi for specifics.

Flowers. Wedding flowers are a wonderful extravagance and a reminder of the first wedding that took place in Eden, where all the blossoms of creation bloomed together. The perfume of the flowers—like the scent of the spice box in the *havdalah* ceremony—is a hint of paradise. *Huppah* poles offer a wonderful opportunity for the creative use of flowers and fresh greens.

In line with the wedding's celebration of life, some couples choose centerpieces of live plants. If armloads of cut flowers adorn your celebration, it is in the best spirit of Jewish tradition to ask friends to take them to a hospital or nursing home after the festivities, to share the joy of your day.

A few brides and grooms send the money that would have gone for floral centerpieces to *tsedakah*. In such cases the tables are decorated with notes that explain, "The money that would have been used to purchase flowers has been donated to ——."

A NOTE ON REMARRIAGE

The Jewish injunction "It is not good to be alone" makes every marriage a cause for celebration. The ceremony for widows, widowers, and divorced people is exactly the same as that for first-time marriages, and while Jewish law mandates three days of celebration after a second marriage (there are seven after the first), there is no reason for a second wedding to be the quiet, family-only affair once dictated by secular etiquette. Especially now that remarriage is an everyday phenomenon in the Jewish community, brides and grooms and their families should feel free to plan their weddings as they wish.

Remarriage may, however, pose some special, delicate problems. Death or divorce doesn't necessarily sever ties to a first spouse's family. Widows, widowers, and divorced people often remain close to in-laws from their first marriages, especially if there are grandchildren. A first spouse's family may view a remarriage as a great blessing or they may feel it as a second loss. Obviously, the decision about whether or not to invite people who were once family depends on your relationship with them. Their feelings, as well as the wishes of your bride or groom and children, should be taken into account. Though it's not always possible, it is best for the situation to be discussed openly with everyone concerned.

Children from previous marriages may be included in

wedding ceremonies in ways appropriate to their ages and emotional responses. Since the remarriage of a parent can be a difficult and confusing event, a child who is reluctant to participate should never be forced to walk down the aisle just because it would look "nice" or be reassuring to the parent and soon-to-be stepparent. Most rabbis will suggest at least one prewedding meeting with the bride, groom, and their children to discuss family dynamics as well as ceremonial roles.

Very young children can be part of the processional and/ or asked to carry important ritual objects: rings, cups, or unlit candles to the *huppah*. Older children might read part of the ceremony: the opening prayer, the first *kiddush*, or one of the seven marriage blessings. Or they might select a poem or even write something to recite under the canopy. Teenaged or grown children can hold *huppah* poles. Since marriages always "wed" more than the bride and groom, rabbis sometimes invite the couple's children under the *huppah* for a blessing on the new family.

PART THREE

*Celebrations
and Rituals*

BEFORE
THE WEDDING

TENAIM:
CELEBRATING ENGAGEMENT

The decision to marry is one of life's momentous choices. Some couples have made it the occasion for a celebration based on the Ashkenazic custom of *tenaim*—literally, the "conditions" of the marriage. Every engagement announces that two people are changing their status; the public declaration of their decision instantly designates them bride and groom. *Tenaim* kicks off the season of the wedding, officially and Jewishly.

From the twelfth to the early nineteenth century, *tenaim* announced that two families had come to terms on a match between their children. The document setting out their agreement, also called *tenaim*, would include the dowry and other financial arrangements, the date and time of the *huppah*, and a *knas*, or penalty, if either party backed out of the deal.

After the document was signed and read aloud by an esteemed guest, a piece of crockery was smashed. The origins of this practice are not clear; the most common interpretation is that a shattered dish recalls the destruction of the Temple in Jerusalem, and it is taken to demonstrate that a broken engagement cannot be mended. The broken dish also anticipates the shattered glass that ends the wedding ceremony. In some communities it was customary for all the guests to bring some old piece of crockery to smash on the floor. There is also a tradition that the mothers-in-law-to-be break the plate—a symbolic rending of mother-child ties and an acknowledgment that soon their children will be feeding each other. After the plate breaking, the party began.

Tenaim is not required by Jewish law, and as family-arranged weddings became a thing of the past, the ceremony lost much of its meaning and popularity. The signing of traditional *tenaim* remains a vestigial practice in some Jewish communities, where the agreement to marry is signed on the day of the wedding itself. Modern reinterpretations of the *tenaim* return the ceremony to its original, anticipatory celebration some months in advance.

The celebration of your decision to marry doesn't "require" that anything be put on paper at all, but some couples have used this occasion to formalize decisions about their married life, including some regarding very specific subjects, such as money management, job decisions in a two-career household, moving to another part of the country or making *aliyah* (settling in Israel), raising children, and agreeing to counseling in case of difficulties. While this may sound very untraditional, in fact, *tenaim* documents have historically included clauses and amendments that reflected current and personal concerns.

A modern document can be written in English or in Hebrew and English and can draw on the language and execution of traditional *tenaim*.* It can be calligraphed, witnessed, and formalized by the act of *kinyan*, a symbolic exchange of some object that seals a contract and effects a change in personal status. Or *tenaim* can be handwritten or typed and entirely original. You can read your "contract" before a community of family and friends at a party or keep

---

* The traditional *tenaim* text is found in the Appendix.

it private. Written *tenaim* might simply consist of letters the bride and groom write and perhaps exchange at their engagement celebration. These could be read the night before the wedding ceremony or on another occasion—a wedding anniversary, for example.

A party to announce the news of a Jewish wedding can be simple or elaborate, formal or casual. Modern *tenaim* celebrations often involve improvisational rituals, sometimes structured around recognizable Jewish symbols, sometimes rooted in family traditions, and sometimes altogether original. Some examples of creative *tenaim* celebrations follow.

An Engagement-Party Tenaim. A close friend decided to give Anna and Jon a party to celebrate their upcoming wedding. Because both of their families lived out of town, the guests at the party were the friends—Jews and non-Jews—who would be most involved in the very participatory wedding they were planning—people who would cook, take pictures, arrange flowers, hold *huppah* poles, and chauffeur out-of-town guests.

After wine and cake, everyone gathered in the living room, where Anna explained a little about the history of *tenaim* and "formally" announced the date—according to both the Jewish and Gregorian calendars—time, and location of the wedding. She said, "There we will read our *ketubah*, hear the seven wedding blessings, exchange rings, and break a glass."

Jon explained a little of the history of the wedding ceremony and said, "Anna and I are choosing to sanctify a new stage of our lives. It's not something we take lightly, and it's not something we can do all by ourselves." He explained: "You will all be witnesses to our wedding. The Hebrew word for witness, *ayd*, comes from the word *od*, which means 'duration.' A witness is someone who perceives an event, retains it in his or her memory, and gives permanence to what is transitory."[1]

The designated best man made a sentimental toast and then repeated the blessing over wine. A pottery bowl, bought expressly for the occasion, was placed inside an old pillowcase, and a special friend was asked to stamp on it. There were shouts of "Mazel tov!"

Later another friend asked Anna and Jon to sit in the center of a circle of their friends. She produced scissors and many balls of colored yarn and asked each person to attach himself or herself to the couple and to tell the story of where and when they'd met, what they had learned from one another, and what the nature of the connection was. After an hour the room looked like a colorful, crazy spider's web. And friends from the different corners of Jon and Anna's lives had become a community that assembled again to rejoice at their wedding.

A Havdalah Tenaim[2] Barbara and Brian knew that circumstances would prevent them from being together for quite a while. They decided to make an agreement, in the presence of witnesses, that they would marry "in accordance with the law of Moses and Israel" within twelve months of their residing in the same household. They promised that until such time they would support and care for each other, visit and communicate as often as possible, and in case of a serious personal problem, they would attempt a reconciliation. They wrote this agreement in Hebrew and in English, with room for their signatures and the signatures of two witnesses.

They sent invitations to friends and family to come and celebrate their *tenaim*. The invitations included an explanation of the ceremony and a quote from Hosea 2:21: "I will betroth you forever. I will betroth you with righteousness and justice and with goodness and mercy." Their *tenaim* was structured around *havdalah*, the ceremony on Saturday evening that separates Shabbat from the rest of the week and that celebrates distinctions. After Barbara explained the history of *tenaim*, she lit two separate candles rather than the customary braided *havdalah* candle.

Brian talked about the contract they had drawn up, and then a friend told a Midrash about how Jacob and Rachel fell in love and made a pact that someday they would marry, no matter what happened to them. "And so the Bible says that Jacob served seven years for Rachel and they seemed to them but a few days because of their love for one another."

Barbara explained that at this *havdalah* she and Brian were making a distinction between a time when they were separate and a time when they would be together. The blessing over wine was sung and translated, and the couple dipped their ring fingers in the wine and put them to each other's lips. The wine was then passed to the people around them.

The witnesses read the *tenaim* document, and it was signed. The *havdalah* blessing traditionally recited over a spice box was pronounced over two fragrant blossoms Brian and Barbara gave to each other as tokens of *kinyan*, which were then passed around the room.

The guests were invited to add their thoughts and blessings, and then the couple took the two candles and together read, "As we bring together the two candles of our lives until this moment, we ask that our bond be as vibrant and as illuminating as this flame, that it continually be renewed by the strengths of our individual selves, and that like this powerful flame, our life together may bring light and warmth and service to our people." They brought the light of their two candles together and recited the blessing over the flame and a final *havdalah* prayer:

Blessed be You, Life-Spirit of the universe,
Who makes a distinction between holy and not yet
    holy,
between light and darkness,
between Shabbat and the six days of the week,
between committed and uncommitted,
between common goals and personal goals,
between love and aloneness.
Blessed be you,

> Who distinguishes between what is holy, and what is
> not yet holy.

Some wine was poured into a plate, and the candles were doused together in the wine. The plate was wrapped in a cloth and broken against a wall to shouts of "Mazel tov!" The Sheheheyanu, a prayer of thanksgiving, was sung. And the party went on into the night.

Barbara and Brian had the pieces of the broken plate mounted and framed. It hangs in their home, a conversation piece that is already an heirloom.

Family Tenaim. Ruth and David came from the same city but no longer lived near their families. When they went home for the winter holidays, they gathered their clans together for the announcement. The news had long been anticipated and it was greeted with kisses and questions. Where? When? How?

After everyone had eaten, Ruth and David asked them all to be seated. Because they came from very traditional homes, Ruth and David agreed that only a traditional *ketubah* would ensure peace during the months of planning. But they had taken the opportunity of writing *tenaim* that spelled out what they saw as their obligations to each other. They agreed to share equally in the raising of children and in the support of their family, and they also promised their best attempts at patience and understanding. David made special provision for a rabbi to act on his behalf to grant his wife a *get*—a religious divorce—in case he was, for any reason, unable to give Ruth a divorce himself. They read these *tenaim* to their families, who were both impressed and a little mystified by the seriousness of their children.

Ruth unwrapped a bowl she had saved from her childhood, and David produced a ceramic cup that was his since he was a baby. They explained the custom and asked their mothers to break them, which both women did, crying and laughing. Everyone was invited to take a little piece of broken bowl or cup as a memento of the evening.

Then Ruth and David distributed paper and pens to the people in the room and asked them to write a wish, or blessing, or memory or any kind of message to each of them. They sealed these in envelopes, which they opened in the hour they spent alone, separately, before the *huppah*.

Finally, one of Ruth's sisters announced her plan to weave a *huppah* for the couple. She brought out rolls of wide pastel-colored ribbon, directed everyone where to stand and when to move, and somehow they managed to create a canopy that shimmered like a rainbow.

The *huppah* hangs suspended over Ruth and David's bed. The letters from their family members—some of whom have died since their wedding—fill a treasured album.

CELEBRATING COMMUNITY

Few marriages are "accomplished" in a single ceremony. From *tenaim* to *huppah*, brides and grooms inhabit a kind of celebratory never-never land filled with special meals and parties. These are occasions for affirming commitments we often take for granted, for celebrating with the different communities we inhabit and depend on.

Celebrating Sisterhood. For women in most cultures marriage has been life's most important rite of passage. The gathering of women to celebrate with, adorn, and advise a bride before her wedding is probably as ancient a custom as marriage itself.

In Sephardic and Mizrachi communities women's parties remain an important feature of wedding festivities. Specifics vary from community to community, but, in general, sometime during the week before the *huppah* the female relations and friends of the bride (and, depending on local practice, the groom's mother, sisters, and aunts) gather to eat, sing, and on the day of the wedding even dress the bride. The songs tend to be playful, romantic, and erotic. The food is abundant, elaborate, and mostly sweet. In some Middle-Eastern Jewish communities the bride's hands and feet are painted with a reddish paste made of henna (a cosmetic dye known to the ancient Eygptians) as protection against the evil eye. The bride is also ritually fed seven times by her mother—a gift of strength, an omen of abundance.

All that remains of women's wedding celebrations in America is the bridal shower, usually a literal showering of household goods: kitchen utensils and linens that essentially "dower" the bride. But toasters and tea towels aren't the only reasons for women to celebrate together. A shower can be an affirmation of sustaining women-to-women relationships in families and among friends—with or without the toasters. When gifts are handmade or representative of feelings and wishes for the bride, bridal showers can take on new meaning.

Whatever the nature of the gifts, each woman could be asked to bring a copy of a photograph of herself with the bride, which might be pasted into a commemorative scrapbook of the occasion. Or an instant-picture camera could be used to snap each guest with the bride, and these could form a souvenir album.

Kitchen showers might feature family-secret or all-time-favorite recipes. A request could be made for kosher dishes or special foods served during Jewish holidays or the bride's favorites—from chocolate to Chinese cuisine. These too could be assembled in an album or card file.

Drawing inspiration from the American friendship quilt, the friend giving the shower can ask each guest to make a quilt square decorated with a design that has some meaning for the bride or that conforms, perhaps, to a particular color scheme. The hostess should designate the size and shape of each piece and allow enough time for preparation. The squares can be sewn together—maybe even at the shower

—to be used as the *huppah* cover and/or as a bedcovering. Extra or late-arriving squares can be used to create a *challah* cover, wall hanging, or pillow.

Of course, gifts are not absolutely necessary. For smaller gatherings, each woman can speak about her relationship with the bride, recalling the first time she met the bride's fiancé, and express her fondest wish for the couple's future. (A tape recording of these words would be a treasure.)

Although *mikvah* is an essentially personal experience, it can also be the occasion for a very special women's party. It is customary among Sephardic women to celebrate the bridal *mikvah*. Musicians are hired to accompany the bride and a singing entourage of female family members and friends to and from the ritual bath.*

Men's Parties. Sephardic and Mizrachi men gather for male-only celebrations that mirror the women's festivities during the week prior to a wedding. Men, sometimes representing three or four generations, eat, smoke, sing, and tease the groom. In some Ashkenazic *shtetls* exuberant friends would carry wedding-bound compatriots through the streets and into the synagogue. Grooms were seated on the *bimah* (platform or altar) under a canopy, and special songs were sung in their honor.†

Stag parties and smokers came into vogue in Jewish communities as the ghetto walls crumbled and customs of the larger culture were adopted. Bachelor parties are infamous for rowdy excess and have not become fixtures of Jewish American life. Today, however, some grooms gather with close male friends and relatives to ponder the meaning of marriage and fatherhood over food and drink. Men who go to *mikvah* before their weddings sometimes bring male

* See "River from Eden" in following section, "Spiritual Preparation," for a discussion of *mikvah* celebrations.
† The groom's table—in Yiddish, *chossen's tish*—which takes place immediately before the wedding ceremony is another traditional men-only gathering. It is discussed in the section "The Wedding Day."

friends with them to witness and help rejoice in that *mitz-vah* as well.

Family Parties. When marriages were arranged, a couple's families were often acquainted long before the ceremony. Today it's common for the parents of the bride and the parents of the groom to meet during the week before the wedding, usually at some kind of meal. These encounters are held at hotels where out-of-town guests are staying, at restaurants, at the home of the bride's or groom's parents, or in the couple's home.

Unlike English, Hebrew and Yiddish recognize the unique relationship between the families of the bride and groom with a special name—*machetunim*. Meeting the *machetunim* is stressful for everyone. There's a Yiddish saying that no *ketubah* is ever signed without quarreling. Weddings mark the marriage of two families—always a tricky business.

Whenever and wherever they occur, the level of anxiety at first meetings is usually high. Will they like us? Will we like them? Will we have anything in common? Parents are often even more anxious than the bride and groom. After all, they have been anticipating this event since before your birth.

Since first impressions can set the tone for a lifetime of family relations, planning for the first meeting is important. Whatever the size or setting of your first family get-togethers, the primary goal is to smudge the boundaries between "his" side and "her" side. Strategies can be as simple as making sure that everyone meets everyone else at a large gathering and that the bride and groom in particular spend five minutes talking to all the principals in his/her new family.

If the wedding is to be held on Sunday, and if the bride and groom have decided against a week-long separation, a Friday-night Shabbat family dinner can begin the festivities on a very warm note. Both mothers can be asked to light Shabbat candles, both fathers to bless the wine, and grandparents can make the *motzi* blessing over *challah*. If the family dinner is held on the Saturday night preceding a Sunday wedding, a beautiful way of beginning the celebration is by making *havdalah*, the ceremony that marks the end of Shabbat.

This was particularly meaningful for Barbara and Brian, whose *tenaim* ceremony was also structured around *havdalah*. (See page 140.) After lighting a braided candle they began the brief service the night before their wedding by saying: "At this time of *havdalah*, the distinguishing between the sacred rest of the Shabbat and the profane creativity of the work week, we distinguish between a time when we were separate, alone, and uncommitted and a time when we will be bonded together eternally. We weave our lives together with the lives of our people at this moment in transition, in anticipation, and in celebration."[3]

A traditional and very effective ice-breaker is singing. In the *shtetl* the prenuptial party was called *zmires*—songs— and wedding musicians were hired to play then as well as after the *huppah*. Some families have a tradition of writing humorous lyrics to popular songs for family occasions, and the bride and groom expect to be melodically "roasted," with special attention paid to how they met, their shared interests, their not-shared interests. The bride and groom can also write songs about their families, about how the printer messed up the invitations, about the trials and tribulations of renting a dance floor, et cetera. Songs don't have to be Jewish; camp songs, show tunes, anything catchy will do.

At a sizable family gathering a master of ceremonies can also be very helpful in loosening people up with jokes and toasts. (The tradition of the *badchan*, or wedding jester, is fully described in the section "Laughter, Music, and Dance.") The emcee at a family party can encourage toasts and blessings, roasting and singing from both sides, and, finally, announce when the party is over and it's time to leave.

At a small gathering of parents and close relations you

might ask people to bring photographs or other mementos of your childhood. As parents share memories of first teeth, first bicycles, and first dates, they may discover they have more than enough in common "to sit down at the table together"—the traditional "prayer" about prospective *machetunim*.

Another way of forging bonds between families is through the ceremonial presentation of special gifts. Although the giving of wedding gifts is thought of mostly as the obligation of guests, for many centuries grooms and brides and their families exchanged presents, prescribed by local custom, as a way of welcoming a new son or daughter into the family. Gifts such as these commonly have some part to play in the wedding and/or for the couple's Jewish life together: candlesticks for Shabbat, a *kiddush* cup, *challah* cover, a Seder plate, and works of art with Jewish themes.

In some communities men didn't wear a *tallis* until after marriage, so a very traditional gift is for the bride and/or her parents to give the groom a prayer shawl. Now that women wear *tallesim* in many synagogues, a prayer shawl may be a thoughtful gift for the bride from her groom and his family. Families might even collaborate on hers-and-his *tallesim*. A *huppah* made of the *tallis* given by a bride to her groom, a groom to his bride, or by the two families to "their" children, adds a personal dimension to the canopy, which symbolizes the new home being established.*

A note about rehearsal dinners: Many rabbis refuse to take part in wedding rehearsals and advise against the practice

---

* A *tallis* can be commissioned by a weaver or handmade in one of a number of simple ways. You can, for example, just purchase a beautiful piece of cloth (traditionally either wool or linen and, according to Leviticus, never a combination of the two), hem it, and then attach the ritual fringes, or *tzitzit*. It is the fringes that transform a four-cornered piece of fabric into a *tallis*. A simple piece of fabric can be embroidered or appliquéd with a design of your choosing. If you purchase a *tallis*, a personalized *atarah*—literally, "crown"—or neckpiece, can be embroidered with a blessing, the name of the groom or bride, or a decorative design.[4]

altogether. They report that it is a time-consuming, usually stressful, and virtually unnecessary step. Besides, the moment a bride and groom enter the *huppah* is unique, one that cannot and should not be practiced. The ceremony itself is very simple, and the order of processionals and recessionals is almost always left up to the couple and their families.

To avoid rehearsals, appoint a trusted friend who will not be walking down the aisle to act as the processional "starter." The rabbi will give that person the cue for things to begin, and then she/he can direct mothers, fathers, attendants, groom and bride to enter at the proper time. In this way the dinner that introduces your parents to each other and/or helps cement their relationship can be free of the inevitable tensions that arise when already nervous people are ordered to march up and down the aisle.

Community Recognition. The Jewish community publicly recognizes and congratulates its brides and grooms. The *aufruf* (or *oyfruf*, depending on your Yiddish pronunciation of the phrase that means "calling up") is a congregational acknowledgment of and blessing over a marriage. Traditionally, on the Shabbat before his wedding a groom is given the honor of the first *aliyah*—the first blessings before and after the Torah reading. Not even a bar mitzvah takes precedence over a groom. As he leaves the *bimah*, children throw nuts, raisins, and candy at him.

In many congregations today both the bride and groom are called up together, where they may share the blessings over one *parasha*—Torah portion. Some brides and grooms study the Torah portion and present a *d'var Torah*—an explication of the text they read. The rabbi then expresses the community's good wishes for the couple and sometimes repeats the blessing called Mi She'beirakh.[5] Candy is thrown at the couple as they leave the *bimah*. (Wrapped candy makes less of a mess and is easier for children to collect later.)

After the service one or both of the families (traditionally, the groom's) provide a special *kiddush,* which may consist of wine and cake, or a luncheon. (This may include a small number of invited guests or the entire congregation.) If the wedding is scheduled for the following day and there is a family dinner to attend that evening, this *kiddush* tends to be brief so that people have time to rest. But if the *aufruf* takes place a week before the wedding, the *kiddush* can be a joyous Shabbat-afternoon celebration, with eating and singing until *havdalah.*

For couples whose weddings take place in a parent's synagogue at some distance, this *kiddush* can be a celebration that includes friends who can't be invited or won't be able to attend. *Kiddush* can easily be organized as a potluck.

Another way of including a whole congregation in the celebration of your wedding is to host an *Oneg Shabbat* after Friday-night services. Generally, an *Oneg* is a brief, informal affair that consists of coffee, cake, and *schmoozing.*

SPIRITUAL PREPARATION

Jewish tradition considers marriage a turning point that gives people the opportunity to begin their lives anew, reborn as pure and as full of promise as Adam and Eve—the first bride and groom. The spiritual preparation for marriage is very much like the intense reflection and soul-searching of Yom Kippur, when all sins are forgiven those who repent or make *t'shuva*—those who literally turn away from error and arrogance to begin the new year with a clean slate.

The fact that weddings are a very private encounter between two individuals and what they consider holy often gets lost in the onslaught of decisions and details that surround the public event. This chapter includes some traditional and not so traditional ways of letting go of the details of the public event and of considering the meaning of the private encounter.

Mikvah. THE RIVER FROM EDEN

For centuries the Jewish bride has immersed herself in a *mikvah*—a ritual bath—in preparation for her wedding. The bridal *mikvah* was a woman's first trip to a place that would be part of her life's rhythms for as long as she menstruated, and for traditional Jews *mikvah* remains a crucial part of married life.*

Fundamentally, *mikvah* is not about "uncleanness" but about human encounters with the power of the holy.[7] The Torah prescribes immersion not only for women after menstruation but also for men after seminal emissions. The scribe who works on a Torah scroll must immerse himself before writing God's name. All converts to Judaism are required to immerse themselves in the *mikvah*, marking their rebirth as members of the people of Israel. And some observant Jews—men and women—go to *mikvah* in preparation for Yom Kippur, when one has the opportunity to become "dead" to past sins and begin the year with a pure heart. There are Hasidim who make a practice of going to *mikvah* weekly in preparation for Shabbat.

According to the Talmud, the ultimate source of all water is the river that emerged from Eden.[8] By immersing themselves in the *mikvah*, people participate in the wholeness of Eden and are reborn as pure as Adam and Eve. *Mikvah* also represents the physical source of life—the womb—from which humans enter the world untouched by sin.

---

* During her menstrual flow and for seven days after, a woman is *niddah* —from the word *naddad*, which means "separated"—and she and her husband abstain from sexual contact. After *mikvah* immersion a woman is no longer *niddah*, and she and her husband are permitted to approach each other again.[6]

For brides and grooms *mikvah* is a physical enactment of the passage from being unmarried to married. Entering the *huppah* is a public declaration of a change in status; entering the *mikvah* is a private transforming moment. Metaphorically, immersion creates newborns—virgins—so *mikvah* can be seen as the demarkation between premarital and married sexuality.

A *mikvah* is any body of *mayim hayyim*, literally, "living water," running water as opposed to stagnant water. Ponds, lakes, rivers, and seas are natural *mikvaot*. For many, *mikvah* in a body of natural water is a more satisfying experience—spiritually, emotionally, and aesthetically—than *mikvah* indoors in what looks like a miniature swimming pool. However, weather or climate or family custom often discourages outdoor *mikvah*.

The act of *mikvah* is very simple, involving two or three immersions in water and one blessing. No rabbi or other religious "expert" of any kind is required. You enter the water nude, spread arms and legs apart, and immerse yourself so that every strand of hair is underwater. The eyes should not be shut tightly. You duck under, looking and feeling as much like a fetus in the womb as possible.

Upon rising from the water you repeat the blessing for immersion:

בָּרוּךְ אַתָּה יְיָ, אֱלֹהֵינוּ מֶלֶךְ הָעוֹלָם אֲשֶׁר קִדְּשָׁנוּ
בְּמִצְוֹתָיו, וְצִוָּנוּ עַל הַטְבִילָה.

Baruch ata Adonai Eloheynu Melech Ha-olam asher kid'shanu, be-mitzvotav vitsivanu al ha'tevilah.
Praised are you, Adonai, God of all creation, who sanctifies us with your commandments and commanded us concerning immersion.

Custom varies on the number of immersions: two are common but three are also traditional since the word *mikvah* appears three times in the Torah. Other prayers may, of course, be added. For brides and grooms the most common addition is the Shehehiyanu, the blessing commemorating significant first events:

בָּרוּךְ אַתָּה יְיָ, אֱלֹהֵינוּ מֶלֶךְ הָעוֹלָם. שֶׁהֶחֱיָנוּ וְקִיְּמָנוּ וְהִגִּיעָנוּ לַזְּמַן הַזֶּה:

Baruch ata Adonai, Eloheynu Melech Ha-olam shehehiyanu vihigianu vikiamanu lazman hazeh.
Blessed are You, Lord our God, Ruler of the Universe, who kept us alive and preserved us and enabled us to reach this season.

Another blessing commonly recited at *mikvah* is the Yehi Ratzon, a prayer for the reestablishment of the Temple, a prayer envisioning a world as whole and pure as you hope to be upon emerging from mikvah:

יְהִי רָצוֹן מִלְפָנֶיךָ יְיָ אֱלֹהֵינוּ וֵאלֹהֵי אֲבוֹתֵינוּ שֶׁיִּבָּנֶה בֵּית הַמִּקְדָּשׁ בִּמְהֵרָה בְיָמֵינוּ.וְתֵן חֶלְקֵנוּ בְּתוֹרָתֶךָ. וְשָׁם נַעֲבָדְךָ בְּיִרְאָה. כִּימֵי עוֹלָם וּכְשָׁנִים קַדְמוֹנִיּוֹת. וְעָרְבָה לַיְיָ מִנְחַת יְהוּדָה וִירוּשָׁלָיִם כִּימֵי עוֹלָם וּכְשָׁנִים קַדְמוֹנִיּוֹת.

May it be Your will, Adonai, our God and God of our parents, that the Temple be speedily rebuilt in our days, and grant our portion in Your Torah. There we will serve You with awe as in days of old and as in ancient years. And may the offerings of Judah and Jerusalem be as pleasant to You as ever and as in ancient times.

Indoor *mikvaot* are maintained by Orthodox communities. (Your rabbi should be able to direct you to the nearest one.) Although brides are sometimes allowed to use them free of charge or for a very nominal amount, most *mikvaot* depend on fees for use of the facilities in order to survive. Ask about the fee (usually due in cash) when you call to make an appointment. (Men's hours are usually far more restricted, so grooms should call well in advance.)

Most *mikvaot* employ an attendant who is universally known as "the *mikvah* lady," and if you've never been to *mikvah* before, it's easy to be intimidated by her. It's important to remember that her function is not to judge but simply to assist one in the performance of a *mitzvah*. By and large, *mikvah* ladies ask no questions.

Although the immersions and blessings take only a few minutes, plan to spend an hour at the *mikvah*. You will be shown to a private bathroom, usually equipped with towels and perhaps even with disposable toothbrushes, kosher toothpaste, shampoo, and hair dryers. (When you call for an appointment, ask what you'll need to bring with you.) The order of your ablutions is entirely up to you. Clean and trim finger- and toenails; clean ears, and floss and brush your teeth. Bathe in a hot tub. If the *mikvah* is not too crowded, soak and relax. Consider bringing some bubble bath and a facial mask, Then shower, shampoo your hair, and rinse thoroughly. Comb all the hair on your head and body in the same direction. There will be a towel or sheet for wrapping yourself before calling the *mikvah* lady.

She will lead you to the *mikvah* and inspect you to make sure you are ready to immerse. (This usually takes no more than a few seconds, and her businesslike demeanor precludes embarrassment.) She will then tell you to immerse yourself and will lead you through the blessings. If you know the prayers, you may be able to convince her that you know the procedure and don't need her supervision. Afterward you return to the bathroom to dress. And that's it. (Of course there are male attendants during men's hours.)

If you decide to go to a traditional *mikvah*, preparation can make the difference between a relaxing, meaningful experience and a confusing, even alienating one. Before you leave for *mikvah* take some time to think about what the ritual means to you.

Celebrating Mikvah. The Sephardic custom of turning *mikvah* into a joyful party has inspired new rituals and celebrations. These can be very simple, involving an intimate dinner for the bride or groom when she/he returns, or they can be as elaborate and creative as you like:

• One bride mystified the *mikvah* lady by arriving with five friends carrying flowers and a basket filled with food and wine. They waited for her in the foyer, and when she returned after immersion, greeted her with songs, champagne, and her favorite sweets.

• One groom gathered his closest friends at an ocean beach on the morning of his wedding. They sang and prayed as he plunged into the surf and recited the blessing. When he emerged from the water everyone sang the Shehehiyanu. Together, singing, they accompanied the groom to his room to prepare for the *huppah*.

• A bride took her three sisters to a nearby pond the night before her wedding. They held big towels as she immersed herself in the water and sang the blessing. When she emerged in the moonlight they took turns drying her, and each sister whispered a private wish for her happiness.

There are many ways to physically commemorate the entry of a bride or groom into a new stage in her/his life, observing the spirit, if not the letter, of the law:

• Although *mikvah* in a bathing suit lacks the symbolic power of nude immersion, it has been done. One group of women gathered on the far shore of a popular swimming hole a week before their friend's wedding. In a circle around the bride, they all immersed themselves. While still in the water each woman in turn wished for the water to wash away one of the bride's self-doubts. Then each one praised the bride for specific abilities, talents, and beauties. (Similar *mikvah* celebrations have been held in private swimming pools and even in hot tubs. At one, each guest offered the bride a burning candle with a personal wish for a future full of happiness and fulfillment.)

• The ritual washing of hands and feet has been an important Jewish symbol for generations. In Genesis, Abraham washed the feet of the three angels who visited him at his tent both as an act of welcome and as a token of his esteem. The daily *mitzvah* of hand washing in the morning and before eating symbolizes the removal of impurity and renewed spiritual integrity.

At one *mikvah* gathering for both the bride and groom, guests poured pure spring water over their hands. As each person poured, she/he offered a wish for the couple's future. The pitcher and bowl, bought especially for the occasion, were given to the couple as a wedding gift.

• In this spirit of "annointing," one wedding "queen" was seated on a special "throne," to which her closest women friends brought gifts of scent. Each one brought a pure distilled oil of a favorite fragrance—rose, musk, apple blossom, lemon, lily of the valley—and placed a drop on her wrist, her neck, or the inside of her elbow. (Since smell is the most ethereal of our senses, the *havdalah* spice box is passed on Shabbat to offer a final reminder of the beauties of paradise. Covering the bride with reminders of paradise enacts wishes for a perfect marriage.)

• Finally, a *mikvah* of song can be created for the prewedding purification of a sister or friend. A group of women arranged themselves in two lines. Humming softly, they raised their arms to form a kind of passageway between them. As the singing grew louder, and when she felt ready, the bride made her way slowly through this birth canal of sound. At the end of the passageway, which was also a bridge, she washed her face and hands from a bowl of water.[9]

Prayers for Mikvah. From the sixteenth to the nineteenth century, hundreds of books full of women's prayers called *tehinnot* were published in Europe. These were mainly petitionary prayers filled with the concerns of daily life and the life cycle of women. There is a *tehinnah* to recite if a child should fall sick, one for an orphan to say on her wedding day, and another to repeat after giving birth.[10]

Tehinnot were also written for *mikvah*. The following prayers, excerpted from a bridal *mikvah* ceremony written by Barbara Rosman Penzner and Amy Zwiback-Levenson, are modern *tehinnot*, a bridge back to the generations of women who preceded us into the water.

> *Now, as I immerse myself,*
> *I begin a new cycle,*
> *a cycle of rebirth and renewal*
> *of Your world and Your people Israel.*
> *I prepare for my new life*
> *and for the sanctification of that life*
> *through kiddushin . . .*
>
> *Our mothers Rebekkah and Rachel*
> *were betrothed and began new lives*
> *at the gently flowing water of the well.*
> *Our mother Yochevet*
> *gave life to her child Moses in the*
> *ever-flowing waters of the Nile.*
> *Our sister Miriam*
> *danced for the saving of lives*
> *beside the*
> *overflowing water*
> *of the Sea of Reeds.*
>
> *Water is God's gift to living souls,*
> *to cleanse us, to purify us,*
> *to sustain and to renew us.*
>
> *As Moses and Aaron*
> *and the priests of Israel*
> *washed with cleansing waters*
> *before attending to God's service*
> *at the altar,*

So I now cleanse myself
before Your altar of sanctification.

I am now prepared to shed
the impurities of my earlier life;
to become one with another life,
to become a creator of new life,
to become a partner in sharing the joys of life,
to teach and to learn
the lessons of married life.[11]

THE MEMORY OF THE RIGHTEOUS IS A BLESSING

If a bride or groom has lost one or both parents, tradition suggests a prewedding visit to the grave(s) of the dead. Far from being maudlin, this practice can be very healing and cathartic at a time when a loss can seem especially keen. "If only she/he had lived long enough to see this . . ."

During the exhilaration of getting ready, there may be twinges of sadness, even guilt, about not mourning a dead relative or intimate friend who would have so loved to dance at your wedding. Taking the time to visit the grave gives the mourner a chance to remember the loss and to forgive him/herself.

If you decide to visit the cemetery, you might wish to take along your spouse-to-be as a way of bringing him/her closer to the parent she/he will never get to know. This can be both a way of giving life to your memories and of sharing a part of yourself. If you're afraid words may fail you, bring a poem your parent liked or something that reminds you of the one who is dead. Tell your fiancé(e) a favorite story about your parent or a story your parent liked to tell about you. If the grave is too far away to visit, set aside some time for reminiscing, leaf through a family photo album, listen to some of his/her favorite music—alone or with your partner.

You are remembered in love.
You are part of the now in me.
  All the good
  All the love
  All the comfort a person can give
Is remembered
  And repeated
  For your sake.
Time changes
Everything passes
  But love
Peace abide you. [12]

There are other kinds of losses which lack religious or social forms of acknowledgment. For people who have been married and divorced and for people whose histories include other important intimate relationships, it can be useful to take time to mourn the formal end of those loves.

ABSENCE MAKES THE HEART . . .

As in many other cultures, it is customary for the bride and groom to be separated for some period of time before the wedding. Since the groom traditionally covers his bride with the veil before he sees her under the *huppah*, this seems less a matter of superstition among Jews than an occasion for serious reflection.

It was long the custom for couples to be apart for a week. Today, however, it's more common for the separation to last only a day or two. Some couples decide to stay apart from the time of *mikvah* until the wedding. (Such a decision obviously rules out prewedding dinners that include the entire wedding party.)

Some people who live together before marriage think the idea of separation is irrelevant if not dishonest, but others find it useful. Between family squabbles and the inevitable last-minute crises, the week before any wedding can cause serious friction between brides and grooms. A brief period of separation may be a welcome tension breaker. It can allow the bride and groom to spend a little private time with family members or friends who've come a long distance. It can also make a little time to simply pause and reflect.

And even the briefest separation heightens anticipation. The Hasidim believe that the point of any fast is the enhanced enjoyment once it is time to eat (or in this case, meet) again.

FASTING

In most Ashkenazic and some Sephardic communities brides and grooms fast on the wedding day. As on Yom Kippur, abstaining from food is an act of contrition for past sins, helping one to enter the *huppah* cleansed of the past. It is said that the people of Israel fasted on the day that the Torah was given to them at Sinai, so bride and groom fast in preparation for their covenant with each other.

The couple break the fast together when they drink from the first cup of wine under the *huppah*. After the ceremony the woman and man, who began fasting separately, will feed each other their first meal as wife and husband, secluded in *yichud*.

Fasting is, however, prohibited on days of joy and semi-holidays, including: Rosh Hodesh, the holiday of the new moon, except Rosh Hodesh Nissan; Issru Chag, the day after the final days of Passover; Shavuot, Sukkot, Hanukkah, and Purim; the fifteenth day of Av; and the fifteenth day of Shevat.

PRAYER

> To pray is to dream in league with God.
> Abraham Joshua Heschel

The prayers associated with weddings are an assorted lot; they include supplication that the caterer will get things right, thanks for having found such a wonderful partner, blessings for the future, and, traditionally, prayers of confession. This last category is part of the cleansing process that includes *mikvah* and fasting. The bride and groom may pray alone, but some rabbis will meet with the couple (individually or together) during the hour before the *huppah* and lead them in a confessional prayer.

It is traditional for brides and grooms to repeat the Yom Kippur Viddui, a litany of sins that is chanted by the whole congregation on the Day of Atonement. The form of the Viddui ("We have sinned, we have transgressed") lends itself to personal and specific versions:

> *I have been quick to anger with my family and*
> *I have been afraid to show them my love.*
> *I have failed to listen to my teachers.*
> *I have spoken too loudly to my beloved.*
> *I have hurt others.*
> *I have allowed others to be hurt without reaching out*
> *   to help.*
> *I have lied to myself and to others.*
> *I have forgotten my better self.*
>
> *I turn to those I have hurt and ask their forgiveness.*
> *I turn to those who have hurt me and forgive them.*
> *I turn within and forgive myself.*[13]

THE WEDDING DAY

Jewish wedding custom includes special ceremonies of greeting and preparation before the *huppah* is raised. Pre-*huppah* festivities also heighten anticipation and set the tone for the whole day. Tradition gives us three such ceremonies: *kabbalat panim* (literally, "receiving faces"), which in Yiddish is *chossen's tish*—a gathering at the "groom's table"; *hakhnassat kallah*—attending or escorting the bride; and *bedeken de kallah*—veiling the bride.

The Groom's Table. All the male guests (or just a small circle of friends and relatives) gather to sign *tenaim* and the *ketubah.* Before the *ketubah* can be signed, the rabbi or one of the witnesses must make a *kinyan*—the ritual act of acquisition—with the groom. Acting on behalf of the bride, the rabbi or one of the witnesses gives the groom some object, usually a handkerchief. By accepting it the groom indicates that he is willing to assume the obligations stipulated in the *ketubah.* Schnapps (whiskey) or wine and cake are served, and the groom may present a *d'var Torah,* a lecture on the weekly Torah portion. But in order to spare the already nervous groom, he is invariably interrupted with songs, jokes, and words of Torah from his guests.

Attending the Bride. While the groom and his friends are thus engaged, the bride is surrounded by women in another room. She may be seated in a special chair covered with pillows or perhaps a white sheet strewn with flowers to receive greetings and blessings from her guests. Unmarried and newly married women sing songs and dance around her chair, and the wedding musicians may make their first appearance here.

Veiling. When she is ready, the bride sends a delegation to the groom's table to invite the men to the veiling, which is the last ceremony before the wedding begins. This is usually the first time the couple has seen each other for a week or a few days. The groom, attended by his guests, enters the bride's chamber, where she is flanked by members of her family or by both mothers or by rows of little girls holding candles. The groom lowers the veil over the bride's face to avoid making Jacob's mistake. (Because he didn't see the face of his bride, Jacob married Leah instead of Rachel, the woman he loved.) By "dressing" his bride with a veil the groom sets her apart from all others.

A *ketubah* signing or veiling attended only by family members and close friends can add a feeling of intimacy to large weddings. Pre-*huppah* festivities also provide ways of giving honorary roles (for example, the pen bearer and the veil carrier) to people who aren't included in the wedding ceremony. The three ceremonies described above have been revived and embellished in great and imaginative variety:

Tish for Two. To begin their wedding Ellen and Mark decided to hold both a *chossen's tish* and a *kallah's tish*—bride's table. Male guests were directed to one room in the synagogue and women to another. Hors d'oeuvres, tea, and wine were served. Ellen's cousin delivered a short speech about the bride's family history, paying special attention to stories about her matrilineal relatives—grandmothers, aunts, sisters, and mother. At Mark's *tish* his best friend spoke about the meaning of the groom's Hebrew name, Moshe, which was also his great-grandfather's name.

Ellen had decided not to wear a veil, so after the two "tables" the couple, their parents, and the two witnesses joined the rabbi in his study for the *ketubah* signing. Meanwhile, as a variation on the "guest book," the rest of the company was asked to write personal messages into a "book of blessings." A shofar blast called everyone into the sanctuary for the *huppah*.

A Lehrnen. Barbara and Brian invited their immediate family and closest friends to a pre-*huppah* gathering they called "the *lehrnen*"—Yiddish for "learning." People gathered around a table in the synagogue's function room, where cake and brandy were served. The couple spoke about the importance of mutuality in their wedding ceremony, and they explained why they had decided to use both a traditional and an egalitarian *ketubah*.

Next Barbara placed a *kippah* (*yarmulke*, or headcovering) on Brian's head. Brian draped the veil over Barbara, and they spoke the priestly blessing to each other. The rabbi explained the meaning of *kinyan*, after which both Barbara and Brian took hold of the kerchief he extended to them, symbolically yet actively consenting to all that was about to happen.

Two of their closest friends, a woman and a man, signed the marriage contracts. The rabbi led the group in some songs, and then family members and friends told stories about the couple until it was time for the ceremony to begin.

The Rose-Covered Kallah. Larry's *tish* conformed to the customs of his traditional family. He prepared a short *d'var Torah* on the Torah portion for the week of his wedding and delivered it to the applause of the male members of his large, extended family. The *ketubah* was signed by two male witnesses at the *chossen's tish*, after which there was something of a "roast," complete with song parodies and silly limericks about the groom.

Meanwhile Suri was in another room receiving the women guests. As each woman came in to greet Suri she was handed a white rose. Every guest whispered her best wishes as she kissed the bride and then placed her rose in one of the vases arranged around her chair. Eventually the bride was surrounded by flowers, which were later transferred to the tables at the wedding dinner.

Although Suri felt extremely fortunate in having so many female relatives on hand for her wedding, she was keenly aware of the absence of an aunt who had died the year before. As a memorial she had had placed above her bridal throne a canopy made of a fine lace tablecloth that had been treasured by her aunt.

The groom was carried on a chair into Suri's room. As

Larry lowered the veil Suri's brother recited the traditional blessing:

אֲחֹתֵינוּ אַתְּ הֲיִי לְאַלְפֵי רְבָבָה.

Achotenu: at hayi le'alfei revavah.

Our sister, may you be the mother of thousands of myriads.

Finally, her father held his daughter's hands as he repeated the benediction:

May God make you like Sarah, Rebekkah, Rachel and Leah.
May God bless you and keep you,
May God make The Countenance shine upon you and be gracious to you,
May God lift The Countenance upon you and give you peace.

Larry's brother helped him on with a *kittel*, and the guests proceeded to the sanctuary for the *huppah*.

Music and Dancing. Helen and Mark were fortunate in having many talented musicians among their friends. Mark and his male guests were serenaded with singing and guitar playing at the *chossen's tish*, while women danced around Helen's chair to the sounds of flute, drum, and tambourine. Mark was brought to Helen by means of a singing conga line, which then circled the two of them.

A traditional *ketubah* was signed by two male and two female witnesses after Mark and Helen accepted a pen from the rabbi as *kinyan*. As Mark lowered the veil and Helen helped Mark into a *kittel* she had made, the musicians played a melody that became the theme of their wedding; the same tune was played as they walked to the *huppah*, and again to accompany their first dance together as husband and wife.

Meditative Moments. Judith and Alan, who had both been married before, decided on a small, at-home wedding. They chose to use the hours before their wedding for reflection and for talking with members of their families. Judith made fifteen-minute-long "appointments" with her mother, father, sister, and daughter. Alan went for a short walk with his parents. Then they met with the rabbi, who led them through a brief meditation.

Judith and Alan wanted their veiling to be an especially intimate event, when they could search each other's eyes before entering the *huppah*. Only the rabbi and the couple's immediate family were present when Alan covered Judith with the lace mantilla he had bought as a wedding gift. The rabbi then spoke of the mystical teachings about veiling: that it gives the bride "special eyes" with which to watch over her children, and that *bedeken* connects her to the future, so that when she walks to the *huppah*, all her children and grandchildren until the end of their generations walk with her.

When the guests arrived the rabbi read the *ketubah*, which was signed by the bride, groom, rabbi, and two official witnesses. A long sheet of parchment was attached to the *ketubah*, and all the guests were invited to sign and become witnesses as well.

All Together Now. When Abby and Jacob were married, the prewedding festivities and *huppah* took place in the same room, in one continuous motion. The rabbi assembled all the guests around a table at one end of the sanctuary and taught them a *niggun*—a wordless melody. As they sang and clapped, Jacob followed his mother into the room. Next Abby followed her parents up to the table. The two witnesses were asked to come and sit with the bride, groom, and rabbi. The first of the two cups of wine was blessed and given to the couple to drink. Then the *ketubah* was explained, read aloud, and signed by the five people at the table.

As Abby removed the blue *kippah* from Jacob's head and replaced it with a new white one and Jacob put a veil on Abby, the couple whispered to each other their intention to enter a covenant with the other and with God.

The *huppah* pole holders were then instructed to raise the canopy, which had been readied in another part of the room, and the guests took their seats around it. Two musicians playing a dulcimer and a concertina struck up a slow, stately melody based on a Yiddish folk song. The groom's mother walked to the *huppah* on the arm of the male witness; the bride's father followed with the female witness; and then the bride's mother and brother walked down the aisle. The bride and groom entered the *huppah* together and the ceremony began.

UNDER THE HUPPAH

A Little History: The Jewish wedding began to take its current shape during the eleventh century. Before that, marriage was accomplished in two distinct rituals, separated by as much as a year. The first of these was betrothal, or *erusin*, also called *kiddushin*, from the same root as the word *kadosh*, meaning "holy." After their betrothal the bride and groom were considered legally wed, and a *get*, the formal bill of divorce, was necessary to dissolve the contract. Even so, the marriage was not consummated until after the next ceremony, *nissuin*—"nuptials."

Nissuin derives from the verb *nasa*, which means "to carry or lift" and may refer to the days when a bride was carried through the streets to her new home. *Nissuin*, which also came to be called *huppah*, is accomplished by means of a symbolic act of intimacy that demonstrates the couple's intention to create a new home and new life. *Yichud* became the accepted way of proving that the couple had acted as husband and wife.

The two ceremonies differ in function and feeling. *Kiddushin* is a legal contract involving the precise formulas and transactions of *ketubah* and *kinyan; nissuin* is a far less tangible process, sealed not with documents but with actions. Betrothal designates the bride and groom for each other only, but nuptials gives them to each other. *Kiddushin* forges the connection between bride and groom; *nissuin*, which can also mean "elevation," connects a husband and wife with God.[14]

After nearly ten centuries and despite the fact that both *kiddushin* and *nissuin* are now carried out beneath the *huppah*, Jewish weddings still show the seam where the two ceremonies were joined. The presence of two cups (or one cup filled and blessed twice) is a reminder of the time when two separate occasions were begun with *kiddush*, the prayer of sanctification over wine.

The separation of *erusin/kiddushin* and *nissuin/huppah* came to an end during the eleventh century for a number of practical reasons. First, two separate ceremonies meant two separate banquets, which imposed financial difficulties on all but the wealthiest. Second, the Middle Ages were perilous times for Jews, and an intervening year could bring deportation or death to one of the parties. If a betrothed groom disappeared, his bride became *agunah*, a woman who was unable to marry. Finally, since many grooms lived with the bride's family before *huppah*, the ceremonies were combined to remove the obvious and understandable temptations of couples who had been promised to each other but were forbidden to touch.

BETROTHAL: THE RING CEREMONY

Most Jewish weddings begin with two introductions. The first extends a welcome to the people gathered, especially the bride and groom. The second is a prayer for God's presence at and blessing of the marriage. Although neither the greeting nor the invocation is required by Jewish law, both have long histories in practice. They also function as a liturgical transition between the commotion of arrival and the ceremony about to begin.

The Greetings. Spoken or chanted by the rabbi or cantor, the traditional greeting comes from Psalms 118:26:

בָּרוּךְ הַבָּא בְּשֵׁם יְיָ.

Barukheem haba'im b'Shem Adonai
Welcome in the name of Adonai

בֵּרַכְנוּכֶם מִבֵּית יְיָ:

Berakhnukhem mi'beyt Adonai
Welcome in this house of Adonai

Since a *huppah* consecrates any place, the second line that refers to God's "house" is usually included even if the wedding is not held in a synagogue.

Some rabbis take this moment to remind the guests that their role at a Jewish wedding is not a passive one; they are obliged not only to rejoice and honor the bride and groom on their wedding day but also to remain a sustaining community for them. Since it is believed that the relationship of bride and groom increases the potential for peace and holiness in the world, rabbis sometimes offer a prayer that the wedding will prove to be a source of blessing for all of humanity.

Invocation. Once the guests have been welcomed, God is asked to bless the wedding. The rabbi or cantor will recite or chant words that "call down" particular aspects of the Divine, usually with the prayer called *Mi Adir:*

מִי אַדִּיר עַל הַכֹּל.

מִי בָּרוּךְ עַל הַכֹּל.

מִי גָּדוֹל עַל הַכֹּל.

יְבָרֵךְ אֶת־הֶחָתָן וְאֶת־הַכַּלָּה

Mi Adir el hakol,
Mi Baruch el hakol
Mi Gadol el hakol
Hey'varesh h'hatan v'hakallah.

Splendor is upon everything
Blessing is upon everything
Who is full of this abundance
Bless this groom and bride.[15]

Blessing for the First Cup. There is a saying "Without wine there is no blessing." Wine is associated with celebrations, festivals, and *simcha*—joy. *Kiddush* is part of virtually all Jewish observance as a prayer of sanctification. Although it is acceptable to use a single goblet that is refilled and counted twice, it is most common to use two cups, which are placed on a small table under the canopy.

These *kiddush* cups provide another opportunity for *hiddur mitzvah* and personal symbolism. The old European custom of creating a special wedding cup or a matched pair of goblets has recently been revived by Jewish artists. Goblets used during the ceremony can become household ritual objects and family heirlooms. Some couples take time to shop for a particularly beautiful cup or two, others use *kiddush* cups that have been a part of their families' observance.

Although the groom and bride may chant the blessing, it has become customary for the rabbi to chant *kiddush* on their behalf, and the couple may respond with an "amen."

בָּרוּךְ אַתָּה יְיָ אֱלֹהֵינוּ מֶלֶךְ הָעוֹלָם, בּוֹרֵא פְּרִי הַגָּפֶן:

Baruch ata Adonai Eloheynu Melech Ha-olam, bo-
rey p'ree ha-gaffen.
Holy One of the Blessing, your presence fills creation
forming the fruit of the vine.

In most cases the wine is not drunk until after *birkhat erusin*—the blessings of betrothal.

Birkat Erusin: The Betrothal Blessings: Since this blessing was once recited a full year before *nissuin*, which finalized the marriage, it included a very specific warning to betrothed couples (the groom in particular) that they are not permitted to approach each other sexually until after the second ceremony:

בָּרוּךְ אַתָּה, יְיָ אֱלֹהֵינוּ, מֶלֶךְ הָעוֹלָם, אֲשֶׁר קִדְּשָׁנוּ בְּמִצְוֹתָיו, וְצִוָּנוּ עַל הָעֲרָיוֹת, וְאָסַר לָנוּ אֶת הָאֲרוּסוֹת, וְהִתִּיר לָנוּ אֶת הַנְּשׂוּאוֹת לָנוּ עַל יְדֵי חֻפָּה וְקִדּוּשִׁין.

> *Praised are you Adonai, Ruler of the universe, who has made us holy through Your commandments and has commanded us concerning sexual propriety, forbidding to us (women) who are merely betrothed, but permitting to us (women) who are married to us through huppah and kiddushin. Blessed are You, Adonai, who makes Your people Israel holy through* huppah *and* kiddushin.

This blessing tends to be translated and interpreted in a far less specific manner regarding *kiddushin* and *nissuin*, often along the lines of ". . . and has commanded us concerning marriages that are forbidden and those that are permitted when carried out under the canopy and with the sacred wedding ceremonies."

Some rabbis read the Hebrew *b'racha* and substitute an English prayer that is only loosely based on the original, for example:

> *You are Holy, Adonai, and Your presence permeates the universe. Through your commandments we share your holiness. You teach us to rejoice with the bride and groom, to celebrate their consecration to each other, to*

witness their vows to each other, here beneath the bridal
canopy. You are Holy, Adonai, and you sanctify the
union of Your children beneath the canopy.[16]

or

Praised are You, Monarch over Time and Space, who
has allowed us to share life through huppah and mar-
riage. Praised are you God, who sanctifies your people
Israel through the covenant of marriage.

or

Blessed be the Infinite, lifting us up through holy cele-
bration and awakening us to seek love and to sanctify
our love through huppah and marriage. Blessed be the
Infinite, making the Jewish people and all who dwell
in the world holy through holy weddings.[17]

After this blessing, wine is drunk. There is some rabbinical debate about who should drink from the cup. Sometimes the rabbi will take a sip and then hand the cup first
to the groom and then to the bride, but generally only the
bride and groom drink. Sharing from the same cup carries
the obvious interpretation that married life halves bitter-
ness, doubles sweetness.

The groom's sip has special meaning. At a baby boy's
circumcision the baby is given a drop of wine, and his
parents pray that his life will include study of Torah, good
deeds, and the marriage canopy. From one covenant to the
next, from one cup to the next, this taste of wine fulfills
that prayer. (This will eventually have similar resonance
for brides, since girl children are now being brought into
the covenant with new naming ceremonies that also incorporate a drop of wine in the baby's mouth.)

If at this point the bride is wearing a veil that covers her
face, it is lifted so she can drink. This can be a special
honor, performed either by the mothers of the bride and
groom or by an attendant. (In a very traditional ceremony
the veil comes down again until the ceremony is over and

she is officially a married woman.) If the bride did not give her bouquet to an attendant before entering the *huppah*, she will hand it to someone before taking the cup.

In some communities the first cup of wine is shared with members of the immediate family and sometimes with close friends. The rabbi or an attendant may even carry the cup to grandparents, who are seated close to the *huppah*. Or the bride will hold the cup for her future in-laws, and the groom will do the same for his.

The sharing of wine with others may be publicly acknowledged by the rabbi:

> Two cups are before you. By your choice, only one is reserved for the two of you alone. You decided to share the first cup with those who have been partners in your lives thus far, the ones who have helped to make you the individuals you are.
>
> We are grateful to you, Source of all Creation, for the loving care and teaching of parents, the ties of heart and mind and memory that link brothers and sisters, and for the friendships that fill our cup to overflowing.[18]

The Ring Ceremony. The groom's giving and the bride's acceptance of a ring is the central act of *kiddushin*. With the ring the groom accomplishes *kinyan* and acquires the bride. Strictly speaking, the groom is supposed to memorize the marriage formula, but in order to spare him any embarrassment the rabbi commonly whispers the words, which the groom then repeats. Because it is essential that both bride and groom understand the meaning of these words, the statement is recited both in Hebrew and English (or whatever language the couple knows best):

הֲרֵי אַתְּ מְקֻדֶּשֶׁת לִי בְּטַבַּעַת זוּ, כְּדַת מֹשֶׁה וְיִשְׂרָאֵל.

Haray aht m'kudeshet li b'taba'at zu k'dat Moshe v'Yisrael.

By this ring you are consecrated to me (as my wife) [19]
in accordance with the traditions of Moses and Israel.

This formula, called the *haray aht*, contains thirty-two letters. In Hebrew, the number thirty-two is written with the letters *lamed* and *bet (vet)*, which spell the word that means "heart"—*lev*. The groom thus gives his heart as he recites the words. One of the explanations for the custom of placing the ring on the bride's right index finger, a practice said to be nearly a thousand years old, stems from an ancient belief that the index finger was directly connected by a special artery to the heart. And so his heart and hers are joined. [20]

There are a number of explanations for the Halakhic preference that the ring be placed on the index finger. Some suggest that this was where rings were once worn; others believe the custom simply made it easier to show witnesses that the bride had received the ring. By taking the ring on her most active finger the bride also demonstrates that she accepts it not as a gift but as a binding transaction. The modern liberal custom is for the ring to be placed on the finger on which it will be worn.

The Bride's Response. The bride is not legally required to say or do anything when she receives the ring. Many traditional Jews feel strongly that the bride should not give the groom a ring or repeat the marriage formula because these actions then appear too much like an exchange and not a *kinyan*, which could jeopardize the Halakhic validity of the marriage.

In many circles today, however, the bride takes an active part in the ring ceremony. Liberal Jews often make the bride's part a virtual mirror of the groom's. She gives him a ring and recites the same formula, corrected for gender.

הֲרֵי אַתָּה מְקֻדָּשׁ לִי (בְּטַבַּעַת זוֹ) כְּדָת מֹשֶׁה וְיִשְׂרָאֵל:

Haray ata m'kudash li b'taba'at zu k'dat Moshe v'Yisrael.

By this ring you are consecrated to me (as my husband) in accordance with the traditions of Moses and Israel.

One musical couple sang *haray aht* and *haray ata* to melodies each one had written and kept secret until that moment.

There are a number of ways to acknowledge the bride's participation—particularly her assent, which *is* Halakhicly required—without making her actions appear to be an even exchange. In some instances the bride gives the groom a ring that is specified as a gift and therefore different from the object used for *kinyan*. Sometimes the bride will give the groom a ring later, during *yichud*.

Whether or not the bride gives the groom a ring, she may make some statement of acceptance. The absence of a specific formula for assent has been interpreted as permission for the bride to respond in her own way, using her own words and/or a biblical quotation. One of the most common responses is a quotation from Hosea: "I will betroth you to me forever. I will betroth you to me in righteousness, in justice, in love and in mercy. I will betroth you to me in faithfulness"; or "I am my beloved's and my beloved is mine. In accepting this ring, I consecrate myself to you as your wife in accordance with the traditions of Moses and Israel."

Vows. There are no wedding vows or "I do's" in the Jewish wedding liturgy. However, since this verbal exchange is such a powerful image in American culture, and since couples often feel a need to say "yes" in the course of the ceremony, many rabbis and couples have added vows, to be spoken either just prior to or immediately following the ring ceremony.

Most rabbis avoid formulas identified with Christian

wedding ceremonies, such as "To have and to hold, to honor and obey." Vows, or perhaps more accurately, "promises" or "intentions," can be very personal. Some brides and grooms compose lists of promises they read to each other. Or you can ask the rabbi to read a series of questions you've written—for example: "Do you, Len, promise to be patient with Rebecca, to laugh at her jokes and to comfort her tears, to live together as companions and lovers?" "Do you Dina, promise to be patient with Roger, to learn alongside him what it means to be human, what it means to love another person for a whole lifetime?"

VOICES OF JOY AND GLADNESS

The ring ceremony completes betrothal/*kiddushin*. At this junction it has been customary, almost since the beginning of the combined betrothal-and-nuptials wedding in the twelfth century, to make a clear separation between the two ceremonies. Traditionally, this is done by having the rabbi read the *ketubah* and hand it to the groom, who in turn gives it to the bride. The bride gives the document to her parents or to an attendant for safekeeping.*

The custom of separating the two ceremonies with the *ketubah* reading is still very much in practice. Often the rabbi reads the Aramaic (or if the text has been revised, the Hebrew), and the bride and groom translate. Sometimes the bride and groom read both languages themselves or forgo the Hebrew version. If the *ketubah* is an egalitarian document that articulates a couple's commitment, they

---

* These arrangements have been extremely important because marriage could not be legally consummated unless the *ketubah* was in the bride's possession.

may read it directly to each other as a very Jewish way of exchanging "vows."

The bride can honor one of her attendants or guests by handing her or him the *ketubah*, and the attendant should be told in advance what to do with the document once the ceremony is over. At some weddings, the *ketubah* is passed from hand to hand; sometimes it is displayed on an easel during the festivities later.

Generally this is when the rabbi makes a short speech. A rabbi who knows you well may be able to express things about the two of you that will be moving and important. If, however, you don't feel much of a connection with the rabbi, you can reasonably ask that she/he not feign closeness and make his/her comments brief. If you'd like to add certain things but are afraid you'll be too nervous to say or read them, you might ask the rabbi to include your thoughts as part of the sermon.

This natural break in the action is a good time for personal additions to the ceremony. Special friends are often invited to read poems, prayers, and parables. Again, the Song of Songs is the most traditional source. A number of original poems composed to honor the weddings of friends appear below.

Although it is considered disrespectful to play music during the ceremony or *ketubah* reading, music can be integrated in the ceremony as a sort of "backdrop" during these readings. As very special wedding gifts, musically talented friends and family members have presented couples with original songs and instrumental compositions to be sung or played under the *huppah*.

This portion of the ceremony can even be extended to include all the guests, who could read responsively or in unison from prayers in a wedding booklet or on sheets distributed before the ceremony begins. But additional prayers, poems, or musical presentations should be kept short. Ten minutes of poetry or song can make the proceedings feel more like a concert than a wedding and overwhelm the liturgy, which is very brief to begin with.

NUPTIALS: THE SEVEN
MARRIAGE BLESSINGS

Nissuin begins with another *kiddush* and consists of the *sheva b'rachot* and *yichud*. Although the seven blessings might seem the more important element, of the two only *yichud* is strictly necessary. A wedding requires only two witnesses to be valid, but you need a *minyan*—ten adult Jews—for the seven blessings.

The *sheva b'rachot* can be offered in any number of ways. It is most common for the rabbi to read or chant them all, first in Hebrew and then in English, but there is also a long tradition of honoring special guests by asking them to read or chant a blessing either from their seats or under the *huppah*. Drawing from Sephardic tradition, parents sometimes come forward to cover bride and groom with a single *tallis* before the seven wedding blessings are recited. The *sheva b'rachot* can be divided and parceled out in any number of ways. They can be:

- read or chanted entirely by the rabbi or cantor.
- read or chanted in Hebrew by the rabbi or cantor with English translations read by designated family members and friends.
- read by married couples who are asked to share the honor of a blessing; one reading the Hebrew, the other, the English.
- read or chanted in Hebrew by the rabbi with the English translation read in unison by all the guests, who are given copies of the text.

The *sheva b'rachot* comprise the bulk of the wedding liturgy, yet only the last two have anything to say about weddings or brides and grooms. Read as a whole, however, they place a particular bride and groom within the context of Jewish time, giving a view of history in which time is not conceived as being endlessly linear but as having a definite beginning and a definite end.[21]

The *sheva b'rachot* mention the beginning of time in Eden, when life was wholeness, and the end of days, when that wholeness will be restored. Since Eden the world has been in exile from the experience of unfragmented existence, an exile that extends from earth to heaven. The Garden was lost, the Temple destroyed, even God is not whole. *Shechinah*, God's feminine self, wanders the earth, cut off, bereaved. God and *Shechinah* are reunited on Shabbat, the day that offers a taste of paradise, as bridegroom and bride.

Both heaven and earth long for a redemption from this exile, a restoration of Edenic harmony to the whole of creation. A wedding is a focal point in history, a fulcrum between the first and the last and the embodiment of union and unity. Since Judaism has no concept of individual redemption, the *huppah* provides the whole community with a glimpse into the blessing of the uncracked, whole reality that was and will be.

בָּרוּךְ אַתָּה יְיָ אֱלֹהֵינוּ מֶלֶךְ הָעוֹלָם, בּוֹרֵא פְּרִי הַגָּפֶן:

You Abound in Blessings, Adonai our God, who creates the fruit of the vine.

The Talmud mentions only six wedding blessings, but since the sixth century, Jews have made a universal practice of adding *kiddush*—the sanctification of God's name over wine—to round the number up to the much more mystically satisfying seven. Seven is the number of completion, the number of days it took God to create the universe.

In addition to being a prayer of sanctification, *kiddush* praises God's creative power. The next three *b'rachot* all celebrate the theme of creation in a sequence that builds to the blessing of marriage. (In some communities the bride's veil is lifted at this point and the couple drinks. However,

it's most common not to taste the second cup until after all
seven blessings.)

בָּרוּךְ אַתָּה יְיָ אֱלֹהֵינוּ מֶלֶךְ הָעוֹלָם, שֶׁהַכֹּל בָּרָא
לִכְבוֹדוֹ:

*You Abound in Blessings, Adonai our God, You created
all things for Your glory.*

The second blessing praises God for having done the work
of creation "in the beginning." For the rabbis, marriage was
considered a testimonial to God's creativity, since the union
of two disparate natures was considered as great a miracle
as splitting the Sea of Reeds. Every wedding goes further
toward completing creation, which is God's glory.

בָּרוּךְ אַתָּה יְיָ אֱלֹהֵינוּ מֶלֶךְ הָעוֹלָם, יוֹצֵר הָאָדָם:

*You Abound in Blessings, Adonai our God, You created
humanity.*

בָּרוּךְ אַתָּה יְיָ אֱלֹהֵינוּ מֶלֶךְ הָעוֹלָם, אֲשֶׁר יָצַר אֶת
הָאָדָם בְּצַלְמוֹ, בְּצֶלֶם דְּמוּת תַּבְנִיתוֹ, וְהִתְקִין לוֹ מִמֶּנּוּ
בִּנְיַן עֲדֵי עַד. בָּרוּךְ אַתָּה יְיָ, יוֹצֵר הָאָדָם:

*You Abound in Blessings, Adonai our God, You made
humankind in Your image, after Your likeness, and
You prepared from us a perpetual relationship. You
abound in Blessings, Adonai our God, you created humanity.*

These blessings acknowledge God's creation of Adam—
humanity. The third, which speaks of Adam as an undif-
ferentiated single entity, is a blessing over individual
human life. In the context of a wedding it invites blessings
on the bride and the groom as separate people.

The fourth blessing extols God's creation of human
beings in the image of and after the likeness of the Holy

One. And in this *b'racha* Adam receives a gift "out of our very self," a "perpetual structure"—love/sexuality/marriage—that keeps humanity alive. Thus it praises the greatest happiness possible in human life—union with another—and blesses the bride and groom together.

The third *b'racha* addresses the creation of the human body, while the fourth deals with the soul, the divine aspect of the human. If creation is understood as an ongoing process, these *b'rachot* are a challenge to fulfill the potential for creativity, blessing, and peace that God bestowed on humanity on the sixth day.

The blessings that celebrate the making of human beings are often read by the couple's parents. This prayer is not recited at the time of a birth because babies are all and only potential; their humanity is still a question mark. By the time of a wedding, however, parents know whether their child has become a *mensch* deserving of this *b'racha*. Reciting these blessings is a way of celebrating a successful parenthood.[22]

שׂוֹשׂ תָּשִׂישׂ וְתָגֵל הָעֲקָרָה, בְּקִבּוּץ בָּנֶיהָ לְתוֹכָהּ
בְּשִׂמְחָה. בָּרוּךְ אַתָּה יְיָ, מְשַׂמֵּחַ צִיּוֹן בְּבָנֶיהָ:

May she who was barren rejoice when her children are united in her midst in joy. You Abound in Blessings, Adonai our God, who makes Zion rejoice with her children.

This is easily the most confusing of the *sheva b'rachot*, the one given the freest translation and sometimes entirely rewritten. Of the many interpretations it has inspired, one of the more common equates Zion with Jerusalem, so the blessing fulfills the verse "Let my tongue stick to my palate if I do not place Jerusalem at the head of my joy." The holy city is mentioned before the rejoicing of bride and groom.

This blessing concretely extends the images of creation and continuity with talk of fertility, of a mother surrounded by children. The fifth blessing promises that God will reenact the miracle given to Sarah and Rachel—that barren women will be blessed with children—thus fulfilling the promise for a "perpetual structure" for the continuation of the Jewish people.

According to Midrash, Zion is the center of the universe, the holiest place. Zion is where Adam was created, where the Temple stood, and where the word of God will issue forth at the end of days. When the messiah arrives—when time comes to an end—the souls of all the Jews who ever lived will find their way back to Zion. And on that day, "when her children are united in her midst in joy . . . Zion [will] rejoice with her children." In a sense the fifth marriage blessing is a prayer for the redemptive unity of the end of days.

שַׂמֵּחַ תְּשַׂמַּח רֵעִים הָאֲהוּבִים, כְּשַׂמֵּחֲךָ יְצִירְךָ בְּגַן עֵדֶן

מִקֶּדֶם. בָּרוּךְ אַתָּה יְיָ, מְשַׂמֵּחַ חָתָן וְכַלָּה:

You make these beloved companions greatly rejoice even as You rejoiced in Your creation in the Garden of Eden as of old. You Abound in Blessings, Adonai our God, who makes the bridegroom and bride to rejoice.

The bride and groom finally make an appearance. The comparison with the joy of Adam and Eve is a wish for perfect harmony; since the first two humans were created of the same dust, theirs was the most compatible marriage possible. The phrase "beloved companions" seems a particularly apt way to think about modern marriages, suggesting the importance of both passion and friendship in marriage.

The sixth and seventh blessings end with references to the couple under the *huppah*. However, in the sixth *b'racha* they are referred to as "bride *and* groom" and blessed separately. Their relationship as beloved companions requires that each be able to stand alone even as they come together, bringing individual gifts to the marriage.

בָּרוּךְ אַתָּה יְיָ אֱלֹהֵינוּ מֶלֶךְ הָעוֹלָם, אֲשֶׁר בָּרָא שָׂשׂוֹן
וְשִׂמְחָה, חָתָן וְכַלָּה, גִּילָה רִנָּה, דִּיצָה וְחֶדְוָה, אַהֲבָה
וְאַחֲוָה, וְשָׁלוֹם וְרֵעוּת, מְהֵרָה יְיָ אֱלֹהֵינוּ יִשָּׁמַע בְּעָרֵי
יְהוּדָה וּבְחוּצוֹת יְרוּשָׁלָיִם, קוֹל שָׂשׂוֹן, וְקוֹל שִׂמְחָה,
קוֹל חָתָן וְקוֹל כַּלָּה, קוֹל מִצְהֲלוֹת חֲתָנִים מֵחֻפָּתָם,
וּנְעָרִים מִמִּשְׁתֵּה נְגִינָתָם. בָּרוּךְ אַתָּה יְיָ, מְשַׂמֵּחַ חָתָן עִם
הַכַּלָּה:

*You Abound in Blessings, Adonai our God, who cre-
ated joy and gladness, bridegroom and bride, mirth and
exultation, pleasure and delight, love, fellowship,
peace, and friendship. Soon may there be heard in the
cities of Judah and in the streets of Jerusalem, the voice
of joy and gladness, the voice of the bridegroom and the
voice of the bride, the jubilant voice of bridegrooms
from their canopies and of youths from their feasts of
song. You Abound in Blessings, Adonai our God, You
make the bridegroom rejoice with the bride.*

In the last words of the final *b'racha* the bridegroom rejoices
with the bride, united in joy, surrounded by ten shades of
joy and a chorus of jubilant voices. Here the ultimate joy
of the end of days and the happiness of this wedding day
become one and the same.

Given the economy of most rabbinic language, the ten
synonyms for happiness in this blessing constitute an orgy
of words, a mantra of the varieties of human joy. The
enumeration of good feeling that ends the ceremony is an
incitement for the guests to live up to their responsibility
to entertain and rejoice with the bride and groom at the
s'eudah mitzvah—the meal and celebration that follow.

TRANSLATIONS FOR THE *Sheva B'rachot*

When it comes to familiar religious texts, standard translations often assume the authority of the original, which is why any English version of "Baruch ata Adonai Eloheynu Melech Ha-olam" other than "Blessed art Thou, Lord our God, King of the Universe" sounds contrived and just plain wrong.

All translation is a form of interpretation. The best translations straddle languages, conveying the meaning, rhythm, and style of the original while achieving integrity and beauty in their own right. Translation demands innumerable necessarily subjective decisions: How should "Adam" be translated? "Man" is a perfectly correct rendering of the Hebrew, but so is "humankind." Why translate "Adonai" at all? Strictly literal translations from Hebrew to English are virtually impossible due to differences in grammar; Hebrew nouns have gender, which requires changes in verb forms. And Hebrew and English deal with tenses very differently.

The following translations of the *sheva b'rachot* include a variety of approaches to the text. All of them attempt to convey the spirit of the Hebrew—as the translators understand it, of course. I hope they will help readers and listeners pay attention to words that repetition may have dulled.

> *Holy One of Blessing Your Presence fills creation, forming the fruit of the vine.*
> *Holy One of Blessing Your Presence fills creation, as all creation reflects your splendor.*
> *Holy One of Blessing Your Presence fills creation, giving life to each human being.*
> *Holy One of Blessing Your Presence fills creation, You created man and woman in Your image, each reflecting the image of God for the other forever. Holy One of Blessing, You give life to every being.*
> *How happy is she who thought herself childless and*

*then finds that her children gather to rejoice within her.
Holy One of Blessing, You make Zion happy with her
children.*

*May these cherished friends rejoice in joy as You once
rejoiced in Your creation of Gan Eden. Holy One of
Blessing Your presence radiates joy for the bride and
groom.*

*Holy One of Blessing Your Presence fills creation,
You created joy and gladness, bridegroom and bride,
delight, song, laughter and gaiety, love and harmony,
peace and friendship. May all Israel soon ring with
voices of gladness and joy, voices of bridegrooms and
brides, voices raised in joyful wedding celebrations,
voices lifted in festive singing. Holy One of Blessing
Your Presence radiates for the bride and groom.*

By Joan Kaye

•

*We acknowledge the Unity of all within the sover-
eignty of God, expressing our appreciation for this
wine, symbol and aid of our rejoicing.*

*We acknowledge the Unity of all within the sover-
eignty of God, realizing that each separate moment and
every distinct object points to and shares in this oneness.*

*We acknowledge the Unity of all within the sover-
eignty of God, recognizing and appreciating the blessing of being human.*

*We acknowledge the Unity of all within the sover-
eignty of God, realizing the special gift of awareness
that permits us to perceive this unity and the wonder
we experience as a man and a woman joined to live
together.*

*May rejoicing resound throughout the world as the
homeless are given homes, persecution and oppression
cease, and all people learn to live in peace with each
other and in harmony with their environment.*

*From the Divine, source of all energy, we call forth
an abundance of love to envelop this couple. May they
be for each other lovers and friends, and may their love
partake of the same innocence, purity, and sense of
discovery that we imagine the first couple to have experienced.*

We acknowledge the Unity of all under the sovereignty of God, and we highlight today joy and gladness, bridegroom and bride, delight and cheer, love and harmony, peace and companionship. May we all witness the day when the dominant sounds throughout the world will be these sounds of happiness, the voices of lovers, the sounds of feasting and singing.

Praised is love; blessed be this marriage. May the bride and bridegroom rejoice together.

by Rabbi Daniel Siegel

•

Be Blessed, O Infinite God, the Power and Majesty of all, creating the fruit of the vine.

We bless You now, Adonai, O Sovereign Spirit of the world, for creating the universe to augment Your glory.

Be blessed, O Infinite God, the Power and Majesty of all, for creating the individual.

We bless You now, Adonai, O Sovereign Spirit of the world, for fashioning human beings who reflect the divine, one at their core, complementing each other in their differences. Be blessed, O Infinite God, for fashioning woman and man.

May our land be happy and rejoice, as a mother whose children return to her in joy. We bless You now, Adonai, for letting Zion rejoice with her children.

Let these loving friends rejoice. May their joy be a paradise on earth. Be blessed, O Infinite God, for causing this groom and this bride to rejoice.

We bless You now, Adonai, O Sovereign Spirit of the world, for creating joy and happiness, bride and groom, mirth, song, gladness and rejoicing, love and harmony, peace and companionship. O Eternal One, our Boundless Power, may there soon be heard in the cities of the world and in the streets of Jerusalem, voices of joy and gladness, voices of bride and groom, the voices of lovers crying in joy beneath their huppahs, of soulmates shouting at their wedding feasts. Be blessed, O Infinite God, for letting this groom and bride rejoice together.

By Rabbi Burt Jacobson

Blessed is the creation of the fruit of the vine.
Blessed is the creation which embodies glory.
Blessed is the creation of the human being.

Blessed is the design of the human being. Developing our wisdom we may become God-like. We are assembled from the very fabric of the universe and are composed of eternal element. Blessed be and Blessed is our creation.

Rejoice and be glad you who wandered homeless. In joy have you gathered with your sisters and your brothers. Blessed is the joy of our gathering.

Bestow happiness on these loving mates as would creatures feel in Eden's garden. Blessed be the joy of lovers.

Blessed is the creation of joy and celebration, lover and mate, gladness and jubilation, pleasure and delight, love and solidarity, friendship and peace. Soon may we hear in the streets of the city and the paths of the fields, the voice of joy, the voice of gladness, the voice of lover, the voice of mate, the triumphant voice of lovers from the canopy and the voice of youths from their feasts of song. Blessed Blessed Blessed is the joy of lovers, one with each other.

Adapted from the *sheva b'rachot* of
Linda Hirschhorn and David Cooper

Translation for the fifth *b'racha:*

Praised are you, Lord our God, who has given us a vision of the paradise we dream of creating with our lives, and called it redemption. We praise you O Lord, who created the commitment of marriage as a foretaste of redemption.

By Rabbi Avram Aryan

FINALES

The Pronouncement. The *sheva b'rachot* conclude the marriage service. Some rabbis make their remarks at this point, but most simply end with the official pronouncement—"By the power vested in me by the state of . . . and according to the traditions of Moses and Israel . . ."—that the bride and groom are now husband and wife. Some add a benediction to conclude the ceremony, which may be the "priestly benediction" asking that God's presence and peace surround the couple and/or a very personal charge to the bride and groom.

The Broken Glass. It may be the best-known element of the Jewish wedding. It is entirely customary and essentially nonreligious. It is a very ancient practice encrusted with generations of interpretation. Few symbols can be given single, simple explanations, but the breaking of a glass at the end of the ceremony may be the most kaleidoscopic of all wedding symbols.

The broken glass is a joyous conclusion that encourages merriment at the *seudat mitzvah*—the meal of rejoicing—to follow. In modern times weddings have become rather solemn, and the shattering gives permission for levity to break out. There is an irony in this, since the breaking of a glass may have started as a way of toning down a particularly raucous wedding party.

It dates back to the writing of the Talmud.[23] "Mar bar Rabina made a marriage feast for his son. He observed that the rabbis present were very gay. So he seized an expensive goblet worth 400 zuzim and broke it before them. Thus he made them sober."[24] Rabina's point was: Where there is rejoicing, there should be trembling.

The custom stuck. By the Middle Ages synagogue façades in Germany were inlaid with a special stone for the express purpose of smashing a glass at the end of weddings. However, the interpretation of the act had changed somewhat by the fourteenth century; it was seen as a reminder of the destruction of the Temple in Jerusalem.[25] Thus even at the height of personal joy the people's sadness was recalled.

This interpretation is still prevalent, although it is often broadened to include all of the losses suffered by the Jewish people. The shattered glass is also seen as a reminder that although the wedding has provided a taste of redemption, the world is still in exile, broken and requiring our care. Its breaking is not only a reminder of sorrow but also an expression of hope for a future free from all violence.

A broken glass cannot be mended; likewise, marriage is irrevocable, divorce notwithstanding. It is a transforming experience that leaves individuals forever changed. It is a covenant between two people and also between a couple and God. In Judaism, covenants are "cut": at Sinai the tablets are broken, at a circumcision the flesh is marked. At a wedding the glass "cuts" the covenant.

The fragility of glass also suggests the frailty of human relationships. Even the strongest love is subject to disintegration, especially since people tend to mistreat their loved ones. In this context, the glass is broken to "protect" the marriage with an implied prayer, "As this glass shatters, so may our marriage never break."

The making of loud noises is also an ageless method for frightening and appeasing demons, who, it was widely believed, were attracted to the beautiful and fortunate—people such as brides and grooms.

The breaking of a glass also has sexual connotations. It is a symbolic enactment of breaking the hymen, which explains why it was considered important that the groom "accomplish" the deed. Any failure was an embarrassing portent of impotence, and if the bride stepped on the glass, the groom's traditional role as *paterfamilias* was threatened. In a more general way, the breaking glass prefigures the intensity and release of sexual union, which is not only permitted to married couples but required of them.

Finally, the glass signals the end of the ceremony. The silence and hush of mythic time under the *huppah*—when the bride and groom stood as Adam and Eve, when redemption was almost tangible—ends with an explosion. People exhale, shout "Mazel tov!," clap their hands, embrace, talk, sing. Breaking the glass returns life to historical time where the world is still in *galut*—"exile"—although a little less broken as a result of the marriage.[26]

There are many opinions and customs regarding which glass is to be broken. According to some, one of the cups used for *kiddush* during the marriage should be shattered, with most opting for the goblet used for *kiddushin*/betrothal. After the *sheva b'rachot* the rabbi can empty the glass into a bowl, wrap it in a napkin, and hand it to the groom and/or bride to break. Somehow the irrevocability of cutting the marriage convenant becomes palpable when the couple crush a glass that helped sanctify their wedding.

It is also common for the couple to provide a third goblet, already wrapped and ready to be broken. This single wine glass can be a special gift from a friend or attendant, or it can be the occasion for a shopping excursion by the bride and groom. (Although a light bulb wrapped in a linen napkin is indistinguishable from a crystal goblet wrapped in a linen napkin, a 60-watt bulb lacks something as a symbol.)

The glass should be wrapped to avoid injuries. Most people simply use a heavy cloth napkin, but some couples make or are given a special velvet pouch for this purpose. Such a bag can be fashioned out of almost any material, in any design, and becomes an instant heirloom.

In order to distance themselves from the sexual conflict and gender arrangements associated with the groom's breaking of the glass, some couples share the act. If a particularly tall wine glass is used, both bride and groom can lower a foot on it. Sometimes the couple jointly holds a covered glass and breaks it on the table under the *huppah* or on a napkin-covered brick held by the rabbi.

The sound is greeted by shouts of "Mazel tov!" and sometimes with a chorus of "Siman tov u mazel tov" as the couple depart. In some communities it is customary to lower the *huppah* over the couple for a moment of privacy immediately after the glass is broken.

Yichud. After they leave the *huppah*, bride and groom will traditionally spend ten or fifteen minutes alone in *yichud*— seclusion. *Yichud* is an echo of ancient days when a groom would bring the bride to his tent to consummate the marriage. Although consummation has not immediately followed *huppah* for centuries, these moments of private time have remained as a symbolic consummation—a demonstration of the couple's right to privacy. (Physical consummation in the few minutes allowed for *yichud* would be entirely out of keeping with the Talmud's insistence that conjugal sex involve mutual consent, gentleness, patience, and joy.)

The word "consummation" means "bringing to completion" as well as sexual union, and *yichud* does provide a few moments for emotional consummation. It is a time to exhale, embrace, and let what has happened sink in. *Yichud* has been described as a period of "bonding." It is also an important respite from the strain of being the center of attention for a whole day. It is an island of privacy and peace before the public celebration begins.

The *heder yichud*, the room in which the now married pair go to *yichud*, can be any private place. If the wedding has been held in a synagogue, the most common areas are the rabbi's study, the bride's room, or the library. In order to ensure the couple's privacy, "guards" may be posted outside the door to keep well-wishers away.

It is customary for the bride and groom to break their fast together during *yichud*, sharing their first meal as husband and wife. There are various customs about what special foods should be eaten. Among Ashkenazim it is "golden soup"—chicken soup, a food that indicates prosperity and builds strength. This may be served in a beautiful tureen, sometimes a special gift from a family member or close friend. In some Sephardic communities the couple is served a meal of doves, symbolic of marital peace.

If neither chicken soup nor doves appeals to you, eat anything you desire. Indulge your whims. Ask a friend to provide a plate piled with your favorite foods: chocolate, taco chips, French bread and butter, whatever. Instruct the caterer, and ask a friend to prepare a tray with some tea and perhaps a sampling of hors d'oeuvres, which you might otherwise not taste. It is traditional for the bride and groom to feed each other during *yichud*, a token that they will sustain each other throughout their marriage. Since most wedding celebrations include wine or champagne, and most couples don't have the time or the inclination to eat much during the meal, it's a good idea to eat something during *yichud*.

Yichud makes it impossible to assemble a receiving line immediately following the ceremony. It is, however, a way of keeping the emphasis where it is supposed to be in a Jewish wedding—on the joy of the bride and groom, not on the expectations of the guests. After *yichud* the bride and groom are announced for the first time as husband and wife. They may be greeted with a toast, with a shower of candy or rice, with singing and dancing.

BLESSINGS
FOR THE SIMCHA

BEFORE THE MEAL

It is customary to begin the meal with a blessing over a wedding *challah*—an especially large, elaborately braided loaf of the egg-rich bread that is a regular feature of the Shabbat meal. There are a number of simple ways to make this brief *b'racha* into a special moment in the proceedings.*

Once the guests have been seated, the bride and groom can make their first appearance as wife and husband and together lead the blessing. The couple might then bring a piece of the *challah* to each table, which, in the absence of a receiving line, gives them a chance to greet everyone personally. Or the *hamotzi* can be recited by parents of the bride and groom or any other honored guests.

---

* Traditional Jews precede the blessing over *challah* with a ritual hand-washing and prayers. At halls that cater to traditional Jewish communities, basins and bowls are positioned around the room or at each table for washing before breaking bread, and again before the *birkat hamazon*, the grace after eating. This ritual also lends itself to a public acknowledgment, as above.

בָּרוּךְ אַתָּה יְיָ אֱלֹהֵינוּ מֶלֶךְ הָעוֹלָם הַמוֹצִיא לֶחֶם מִן

הָאָרֶץ:

Baruch ata Adonai, Eloheynu Melech Ha-olam,
hamotzi lechem min ha-aretz.

Praised are you Adonai, Ever-caring Infinite Being,
Our God, who brings bread from the earth.

One way to begin the meal with "words of Torah" is to
pause over this everyday blessing to reflect on the bounties
of this day.

Baruch ata Adonai

We open our senses to the blessings of the world around
us.

Eloheynu melech ha-olam

We remember creation and the Creator.
We acknowledge that there is a source of power and
purpose beyond ourselves.

Hamotzi lechem min ha-aretz

The Infinite One created this bread.
The bread comes from the earth,
nourished by generations of matter, organic and
inorganic.
It has passed through stages from seed to fruit.
It has passed through many hands and lands.
It has been planted, reaped, threshed, and ground into
flour.
transported, baked, packaged and purchased.
It has been touched
by men and women,
some fat, some thin,
some black, some white,
some wise, some foolish.

Before we eat, we remember them all
and recall our duty to return the gift,
to return the energy about to be created,
to build, to care and to serve.[27]

Sheva Shevahot. According to tradition, only men are counted in the *minyan*, only men may serve as witnesses, only men chant the *sheva b'rachot*, both under the *huppah* and following the wedding feast. While many Orthodox and some Conservative women are not comfortable breaking with these traditions, the need to honor and include their female relatives and friends at wedding celebrations has prompted the creation of an entirely new ritual form: *sheva shevahot*—seven praises.[28]

Drawing on the biblical examples of Miriam, who gathered the women of Israel to celebrate the Exodus from Egypt, and Devorah, who judged and claimed victories in poems and songs, the seven praises are a way of giving voice to women's joy and gladness. Paralleling the *sheva b'rachot* that will follow the meal, *sheva shevahot* are recited before the meal. The seven praises can mirror the themes of the *sheva b'rachot*, or they may concentrate on the bride and groom, honoring their names, their abilities, their plans. Psalms and poems, lines from Song of Songs, and references to biblical foremothers are common resources: "And Miriam the prophetess, the sister of Aaron, took the timbrel in hand; and all the women went after her with timbrels and with dances" (Exodus 15:20). Shehehiyanu, the familiar and powerful prayer of thanksgiving for new blessings, is often used as the seventh praise.

CONCLUDING THE FESTIVITIES

Weddings tend to fizzle to their conclusions; guests trickle out the door, the bride and groom wonder when it's permissable for them to leave. The traditional way to end a *s'eudat mitzvah* is by chanting *birkat hamazon*, the blessings after the meal, which closes the day with spirit, dignity, and finality.

When three or more are gathered at the table, the prayer is sung by everyone present, responsively and in unison. If guests are familiar with the words and melodies of *birkat hamazon*, this can be a powerful affirmation of love and community. If, however, you and/or many of your guests are unfamiliar with the Hebrew prayers, they can be chanted or read in English, or even adapted and amended.

Booklets called *benchers* containing the *birkat hamazon* are distributed to the guests at some point late in the day. (*Benchen* is Yiddish for praying, particularly prayers after eating.) Wedding *benchers* often bear the bride and groom's names and the date, and recently the *birkat hamazon* has become part of a "program" for the wedding service and celebration. Different kinds of *benchers* can be purchased at Jewish book stores; some are entirely in Hebrew, though some provide the English translation and many include traditional songs. Or you can create a *bencher*, with a translation and songs of your own choosing. The *birkat hamazon* is found in most *siddurim* (daily prayerbooks). One translation appears at the end of this section.

As the celebration begins to wind down, a designated leader (or small group of leaders) invites the guests to open their *benchers* for *birkat hamazon*. People usually return to their tables for *benching*, but sometimes a small table at which the bride and groom are seated will be set up in the middle of the dance floor, and everyone gathers around them for the final prayers of the day.

After *birkat hamazon* at weddings, the seven marriage blessings are repeated, except that this time the blessing over wine is read last. The blessings are often distributed among special people who did not participate under the *huppah*. (Such an honor should never come as a surprise; inform the people you select well in advance.) Each *b'racha* can be shared between a couple or a pair of friends, one of whom chants the Hebrew while the other reads an English translation.

And finally, it is traditional to end with the ceremony of the cups. A full goblet of wine is held aloft by a leader of the *benching* during *birkat hamazon*. A second goblet is poured before the *sheva b'rachot* are sung again. With the words "bo-rey p'ree ha-gaffen," wine from both cups is mixed in a third goblet, from which the bride and groom drink. This third cup may then be shared with the couple's parents and/or passed around the room.

This "cup of blessing" represents the combined joy of bride and groom, the completion of both betrothal and nuptials, the establishment of a new entity—a marriage in which all elements are shared. It is a pouring of two lives into one, a hope for future generations, for the unification of all apparent opposites.

The *kiddush* cups used under the *huppah* are usually incorporated into this ceremony, and some couples purchase a third, large goblet for mixing the wine together. This goblet can become a family treasure, used for Elijah's cup at Passover seders. It can also be the cup with which children are welcomed into the covenant at birth.

Benching for Beginners. Birkat hamazon is not a spectator sport. Even if a majority of guests are unfamiliar with Hebrew, it can be orchestrated so that everyone can participate. Hebrew can be integrated in a number of ways into *benching* that is mostly English. One person can lead the Hebrew-speaking guests in the chanting while another person leads the rest of the company through the same passage in English, or sections can be alternated in Hebrew and English.

If you want to encourage guests to offer personal blessings during the *harachamon* (petitionary prayers that begin with the word *harachamon*) portion of the *benching*, it's a good idea to warn them (or at least warn a dependable cadre) well in advance. Then, when the leaders ask for prayers from the company, there can be a "spontaneous" outpouring of good wishes. Or every table might be asked to compose a collective wish on a particular theme: health, home, livelihood, prosperity, peace, children, and so on. A notecard with a specific "assignment" for each table will facilitate this.

Couples who are unfamiliar with *benching* have designed concluding ceremonies inspired by tradition. At one wedding the couple asked four friends to read the four main blessings of the *birkat hamazon* with some personal comments about them. The seven marriage blessings were then read in unison by all the guests, and two cups of wine were mixed in a large pewter cup of blessings. Finally, the guests were asked to stand in a circle surrounding the couple in the twilight outside the synagogue. A friend played an Israeli melody on the flute, and a glowing candle was passed from hand to hand, illuminating smiling faces that shone wordless blessings on the bride and groom. As they left the charmed circle of their family and friends, the light was extinguished in their cup of blessings, concluding the public celebration and beginning their married life.

At another wedding, guests arranged their chairs into a circle around a pair of wedding "thrones"—two armchairs decorated with pillows and streamers. A guitar-strumming friend taught everyone the melody to "Dodi Li," an Israeli folk song based on Song of Songs. As the singing grew louder, the bride and groom entered the circle and were seated on their thrones. As guests continued to hum, individuals came forward to offer blessings and good wishes. Some people had written poems, others simply kissed the bride and groom. After everyone who wished to had come forward, the couple expressed their thanks and left, showered by colored streamers, confetti, and rice.

BIRKAT HAMAZON—
BLESSINGS AFTER THE MEAL[29]

The blessings consist of four benedictions on different themes: thanking God who provides food; blessing the land that produces it; expressing hope for the rebuilding of Zion; and attesting to God's goodness and love. These are followed by a series of petitions generally called the *harachamons*, each of which begins with that word, which means "O Merciful One." (The *harachamons* are sometimes changed to suit the occasion.) Verses from psalms follow, and the *birkat hamazon* ends with a prayer for peace. On joyful occasions the *birkat hamazon* is preceded by Psalm 126.

PSALM 126: A REACHING-UP SONG

When God returned us
To Zion from exile,
We thought we were dreaming.
Then our mouths filled with laughter
And cheers were on our tongue.
The other nations saw and said,
"The Lord has done great things for them."
The Lord has done great things for us,
And we were very glad.
Return us again to freedom, Adonai,
Like streams, long dry, to the Negev returning.
Those who sow in tears
Will reap in joy.
The farmer wants to weep
When he buries the precious seed,
But singing he comes back
With his arms filled with grain.

The Invitation and Consent

> LEADER: *Friends! Let us give thanks!*
> COMPANY: *May God's name be praised now and*
> *forever!*
> LEADER: *With your consent, then, let us praise God*
> *from whose abundance we have eaten.*
> COMPANY: *Praise God from whose abundance we*
> *have eaten and by*
> *whose goodness we live.*
> ALL: *Praise God, Praise God!*

Blessing for Food: *Birkat Hazan*

> *Holy One of Blessing, Your Presence fills creation,*
> *You nourish the world with goodness*
> *and sustain it with grace, loving kindness and mercy.*
> *You provide food for every living thing because*
> *You are merciful. Because of Your great goodness,*
> *the earth yields its fruit. For Your sake*
> *we pray that we shall always have enough to eat,*
> *for You sustain and strengthen all that lives and*
> *provide food for the life that You created.*
> *Holy One of Blessing, You nourish all that lives.*

Blessing for the Land: *Birkat Haaretz*

> *We thank You, God, for the good land that you gave*
> *to our parents as a heritage; for liberating us from*
> *the soft slavery of Egypt; for the Covenant You sealed*
> *in our flesh; for the Torah that You teach us; for the*
> *laws that You reveal to us; for the life that*
> *You have given us and for the food which nourishes*
> *and strengthens us each day; even as it does right now.*
> *We thank You, God, for all Your gifts*
> *and praise You, as all who live must praise You each*
> *day;*
> *for You teach us in your Torah: "When you have*
> *eaten*
> *your fill, you shall praise God for the*
> *good land that God has given you."*

Holy One of Blessing,
we thank You for the land and its fruit.

BLESSING FOR JERUSALEM: *Birkat Yerushalayim*

Oh God, have compassion on Israel, Your people;
on Jerusalem, Your city; on Zion, the home of Your
glory;
on the royal house of David, Your anointed, and
upon the great and holy Temple that was called
by Your name. Dear God, tend us, nourish us, sustain
us
and support us; and, dear God, relieve us soon from
all of our troubles. O God, let us never depend upon
the charity of our fellows, but let us depend on
Your generous help alone, so that we may never be put
to shame.

[If the meal occurs on Rosh Hodesh (the new moon), additional verses found in the prayer book appear here.]

And build Jerusalem, the holy city, soon, in our day!
Holy One of
Blessing, Your compassion builds Jerusalem.

THE BLESSING OF GOODNESS: *Birkat Hatov V'hametiv*

Holy One of Blessing, Your Presence fills creation,
You are our Redeemer, our Maker, our Holy One,
the Holy One of Jacob. You are the Shepherd of Israel,
the good Sovereign, who does good for all. As You do
good each day, so, we pray, do good things for us.
As You provide for us each day, so, we pray, treat us
with loving kindness and compassion, relieve us from
our troubles and grant us prosperity and redemption,
consolation, sustenance and mercy: a good and peaceful
life.
Never withhold Your goodness from us.

THE HARACHAMON PETITIONS

May the Merciful One rule over us now and forever!
O Merciful One, You are praised in the heavens as
You are

praised on earth.
O Merciful One, You will be praised by every
  generation and
You will be honored among us forever.
May the Merciful One deliver us from oppression and
  give us freedom.
May the Merciful One bless this house and all who
  have shared our meal.
May the Merciful One send Elijah the prophet,
may he be remembered for good,
to bring us the good news of redemption and
  consolation.
May the Merciful One bless us and all who are dear to
  us with the
perfect blessing that God bestowed on our parents,
  Abraham and
Sarah, Isaac and Rebecca, and Jacob, Leah and
  Rachel.
May we be worthy of peace, O God, and the blessings
  of justice
from the God of our salvation and may we find grace
  and
understanding in the sight of God and all peoples.

Additional blessings for Rosh Hodesh may be included at this point—for example: "May the Merciful One renew for us this month goodness and blessing."

Petitionary prayers of all kinds are commonly added here: prayers for peace in the land of Israel, prayers for the redemption of Soviet Jews, prayers for brotherhood between Jews and Arabs ("the children of Isaac and the children of Ishmael"), and prayers for world peace. In the spirit of the day, the leader of the *benching* might add special personal *harachamons* as well—for example:

> *May the Merciful One bless Hannah and David with*
> *shalom in their hearts and under their roof.*
> *May the Merciful One bless the parents of Hannah*
> *and the parents of David with many more years of joy*
> *and* naches *from their children.*

*May the Merciful One bless Hannah and David with
a sense of humor in times of minor difficulties and with
patience in times of distress.*

*May the Merciful One bless this company, and allow
us all to gather soon and often for such joyous occasions.*

The *birkat hamazon* then continues:

*May Merciful God find us worthy of
the Messiah and of life in the world to come.
You are a tower of strength to Your king
and are compassionate to Your anointed, David,
and his descendants now and forever.
May God, who makes peace on high,
bring peace to us and to all Israel.*

Many people choose to end the *birkat hamazon* here, with
this prayer for peace. The last two lines are set to a lively
melody familiar to many Jews. The transliteration of these
lines can encourage a particularly participatory and upbeat
conclusion to the *benching:*

*Oseh shalom bimromav, hu ya-seh shalom
Alienu v'al kol Yisroel v'rimeru, Omein.*

But a complete rendering of the *birkat hamazon* continues
with the following, which consists of a collection of verses
from Psalms:

*Fear God, you holy ones,
for those who fear God will feel no want.
Even the strong may lack and hunger
but those who seek God will lack for nothing that is
     good.
Let us thank God, for God is good.
Your compassion endures forever. You open Your hand
and satisfy every living thing with favor.*

You who trust God are blessed, for God will protect
    you.
I have been young and now I am old,
yet never have I seen the righteous abandon those who
    lack bread.
God will give strength to God's people
God will bless the people with peace.

PART FOUR

Husbands and Wives

LIVING AS
BRIDE AND GROOM

When a man takes a new wife, he shall be deferred
from military duty, he shall not be charged with any
business. He shall be free for his house one year and
shall cheer his wife, whom he has taken.

Deuteronomy 24:5

Sheva B'rachot: A Week for Celebration: For many generations brides and grooms spent their first week of marriage
surrounded by their communities, entertained and fed for
a full week at special, festive meals also called *sheva
b'rachot.** A *minyan*—a gathering of ten observant Jews—
assembled every evening and, after eating, repeated *birkat
hamazon*. If at least one *panim chadashot*—"new face"—was
present, the seven marriage blessings were also repeated.
These parties often lasted late into the night and eventually
included nearly everyone in the community.

* The seven days of community participation following a wedding correspond to the seven days after a death. Both are perceived as periods of
transition when people are vulnerable and in need of community "protection" against what were once called "evil spirits," but which could be
given other names. Any major life change provokes anxiety. After a
death one needs protection against despair. When a bride and groom
were barely acquaintances before their wedding, a couple needed support through their initial shyness, awkwardness, and more than occa-
sional panic. Like *shiva*, the seven days of mourning, *sheva b'rachot* lets a
couple know they are not alone in their undertaking.

Although some traditional couples postpone their wedding trips for a week in order to celebrate with family and friends, the get-away honeymoon has by and large displaced the custom of *sheva b'rachot*. However, some couples with large, far-flung families spend the first week of their honeymoon taking the *sheva b'rachot* "on the road." Sometimes an *aliyah* and *kiddush* are organized at a home-town synagogue, or a party is hosted by relatives.

The First Year. Since biblical times the special status of "bride and groom" has lasted for a full year—a year full of changes and congratulations. It is a year for bonding and growth, sharing and learning. The year-long public recognition of the special status of brides and grooms is a way for the community to savor their joy and share their happiness.

The designations "husband" and "wife" really apply only after that first year, when a home is established and, as the Torah suggests, the couple have consummated many aspects of their relationship. A year's seasons and a full cycle of Jewish holidays are shared as bride and groom: a first springtime and Pesach, a first autumn and Yom Kippur.

A JEWISH HOME

When the world was created,
God made everything a little bit incomplete.
Rather than making bread grow out of the earth,
God made wheat grow so that we might bake it into
  bread.
Rather than making the earth of bricks,
God made it of clay
so that we might bake the clay into bricks. Why?

So that we might become partners
in completing the work of creation.

From the Midrash [1]

According to the Zohar, the central book of Jewish mysticism, God creates new worlds constantly by causing marriages to take place. The venue of each of these new worlds
is a home, which is symbolically established by a *huppah*.
But a *huppah* is an outline that needs to be filled, shaped,
and named by the people who have chosen to inhabit it,
"its few lines a sketch for what might be." [2]

For traditional Jews Halakhah provides a fairly straightforward description of the Jewish home: it has a kosher
kitchen, its doorposts are marked with *mezuzahs*, Shabbat
and the holidays are celebrated according to Jewish law,
sexual relations between husband and wife are regulated by
the laws of *taharat hamishpachah*—the laws of family purity.
For the traditional Jew observance of the laws is a daily act
of faith and a method for living a meaningful and examined
life.

For liberal Jews the definition of a Jewish home is more
problematic. Can it be a Jewish home if non-Jews live
under the same roof with Jews who light Shabbos candles
and observe the holidays? Is it a Jewish home if Shabbat
candles are never lit, but the Jews who live there volunteer
unselfishly on behalf of the liberation of Soviet and Ethio-
pian Jewry? Is it a Jewish home if great amounts of money
are given to the Jewish community while bacon fries in the
kitchen? Is it a Jewish home if no one ever gives the question a thought?

One *ketubah* describes the commitment to establishing a
Jewish home as a pledge to be "open to the spiritual potential in all life wherein the flow of the seasons and the passages of life are celebrated through the symbols of our
Jewish heritage. A home filled with reverence for learning,
loving, and generosity. A home wherein ancient melody,

candles and wine sanctify the table. A home joined ever more closely to the community of Israel."[3]

A wedding marks a Jewish beginning, a time for experimenting with the varied forms—the "flavors"—of Jewishness. Bride and groom invariably have somewhat different notions about observance and affiliation, which probably means searching out a middle path and agreeing to follow divergent routes from time to time.

Some of the elements that constitute a Jewish home include: the presence of ritual items (a *mezuzah* at the door, Shabbat candlesticks, a *kiddush* cup, and so on); observance of Shabbat and the holidays; observance of *kashrut;* Jewish books and a reverence for learning; *tsedakah*—charity—given within the Jewish community as well as to ecumenical causes; *hachnasat orchim*—hospitality; affiliation with a synagogue, *havurah*, and/or other Jewish organizations. These and others are generally addressed by rabbis during premarital meetings, not as a laundry list of do's and don'ts but as a prospectus for a life-long exploration of Jewishness. A Jewish home is not a static entity; it changes.

The Jewish home is sometimes called a *mikdash ma'at*—a little sanctuary. It is a powerful image. A sanctuary feels different from a place of business. Sanctuaries elicit different moods and emotions from those aroused by hotel lobbies. Sanctuaries invite a quality of self-consciousness that is not similarly invited by supermarkets. The threshold of a *mikdash*, marked by a *mezuzah*, creates a separation that defies the modern notion that all places are essentially the same, that space is empty of meaning.

In most spaces, doing is primary; productivity is key. In a sanctuary, doing without being is insufficient. "Judaism is not interested in automatons." Like marketplaces and auditoriums, sanctuaries invite people to enter, but for unquantifiable encounters. Sanctuaries affirm that community is as necessary as bread.

Sanctuary is a place of rest, safety, and asylum. The place that by definition, will shelter the dispossessed, feed the hungry, and allow the possibility that *this* wandering beggar may be Elijah, who will never announce redemption if he is mistreated here. Sanctuaries are never closed to people who come honestly, openly, seeking, which is why the sanctuary's money is given freely where it is needed.

The *mikdash* is a place of books but it is no library. Discussion, debate, even loud disagreements are welcome here.

Sanctuaries are visibly different from other places. They are marked off by symbols—*mezuzahs*, candles, special cups, works of art. They are filled with voices, sometimes reading in unison and sometimes in a disjointed chorus. There is music in the sanctuary and occasionally the deep, living silence of a garden.

No synagogue sanctuary is perpetually filled with all the meaning and being it is called to. No home is every fully or finally a sanctuary. There are only degrees of intention.

TAY-SACHS DISEASE

Tay-Sachs disease is an inherited disorder of the nervous system that is one hundred times more common in Jewish children than in non-Jewish children. By the age of about six months a baby with Tay-Sachs disease loses physical skills, sight, and the ability to smile or eat. There is no known cure for Tay-Sachs disease, and death occurs by three or four years of age.

The cause of Tay-Sachs disease is the absence of a vital enzyme called hexosaminidase A (Hex A), which the body requires to break down fatty substances (lipids) in the brain. Without the Hex A enzyme, lipids accumulate, impairing and ultimately destroying brain function. Carriers can be detected by means of a special blood test to determine the enzyme level of Hex A. This involves a complicated procedure, which is performed only in specialized centers located throughout the United States.

If only one parent is found to be a carrier, the couple cannot produce a Tay-Sachs child. However, when both parents carry the gene for Tay-Sachs, there is a one-in-four chance that a pregnancy will result in an afflicted baby. *Since approximately one of every twenty-five Jews of Ashkenazic (Central and East European) descent is a carrier of the Tay-Sachs gene, and fully 90 percent of the American Jewish population is Ashkenazic, it is important that Jewish couples be tested for Tay-Sachs.*

If both parents are found to be carriers, amniocentesis (removal of a small quantity of fluid from the uterus during the fourteenth to sixteenth week of pregnancy) will detect whether or not the fetus has Tay-Sachs disease. The pregnancy may then be terminated.

Most rabbis have information about local resources and encourage genetic testing for Tay-Sachs to be done at the same time as state-mandated blood tests for venereal disease and rubella immunity (for women).

For more information about Tay-Sachs disease and the location of Tay-Sachs testing facilities, write or phone:

The National Tay-Sachs and Allied Diseases Association
92 Washington Avenue
Cedarhurst, NY 11516
Telephone: (516) 569–4300

DIVORCE

According to the Talmud, when a marriage is dissolved, "even the altar sheds tears."[4] Divorce has, however, been a fact of Jewish life since the Torah. In its attempt to sanctify all aspects of human experience, Jewish law is as concerned with the dissolution of marriage as with its creation.

A traditional Jewish divorce involves the writing of a formal document called a *get*, which is commissioned by the husband, delivered to the wife, and acknowledged by a *bet din*, a rabbinical court. While there are a few cases in which a wife can obtain a *get* or compel her husband to give her one, divorce, like marriage, is essentially a male prerogative that requires the man to take action. A marriage that has not been dissolved "according to the traditions of Moses and Israel" is considered binding on the woman.

A woman who hasn't obtained a *get*—even if she has been granted a civil divorce—may not remarry as a Jew. She is called *agunah*—literally, "one who is chained." If she remarries—under any religious or secular authority—her children will be illegitimate *(mamzerim)* and, according to Jewish law, may never marry Jews. (Again, this is not the case for husbands, whose subsequent children, born of Jewish wives, are legitimate.)

Orthodox and many Conservative rabbis will not officiate at a second marriage without first having ascertained that the divorced parties have obtained a *get*. People rarely go through the procedure until one of them (usually the woman) is thinking of remarriage, and then usually if children are planned.

A traditional *get*, like a traditional *ketubah*, is written in Aramaic. It must be executed by a *sofer*, a professional scribe, and it must be absolutely clear in meaning.

TRADITIONAL *GET*

On the ___ day of the week, the ___ day of the month of ___ in the year ___ from the creation of the world according to the calendar reckoning we are accustomed to count here, in the city _____ which is located on the river _____ and _____, I do willingly consent, being under no restraint, to release, to set free, and put you aside, my wife _____ daughter of _____ who are today in the city of _____, which is located on the river _____ and _____, who has been my wife. Thus do I set free, release you and put you aside, in order that you may have permission and the authority over yourself to go and marry any man you may desire. No person may hinder you from this day onward, and you are permitted to every man. This shall be for you a bill of dismissal from me, a letter of release, and a document of freedom, in accordance with the laws of Moses and Israel.

Signed by two witnesses:

Once the wife (or her proxy) has accepted the *get*, she gives it to a *bet din*, which in turn gives her a document stating that she is divorced according to Jewish law and free to remarry. The *get* is then symbolically torn (the covenant is nullified) and kept on file.

Non-Orthodox American Jews who contemplate settling in Israel sometimes seek an Orthodox *get*. In Israel, where Orthodox rabbinical courts are the civil authority for marriage and divorce law, the children of a woman considered *agunah* sometimes have difficulty getting licenses to marry other Jews. (Israeli military men commonly have a *get* written in advance in case they should ever be "missing in action" for a long period of time.)

The American Orthodox community is anxious to expedite the writing of *gittim* (plural of *get*), and accordingly make it as easy as possible for couples to obtain them. Local rabbis—of any branch of Judaism—should be able to help you contact the proper authorities.[5]

Non-Orthodox Responses. Despite its importance in Jewish law, no more than 10 percent of divorced Jews seek a *get*.[6] Since somewhere between one third and one half of all Jewish marriages end in divorce, it appears that most American Jews consider civil divorce sufficient and valid. The Conservative and Reform movements have dealt with the issue in different ways.

Conservative Judaism seeks to adhere to Halakhic divorce law and empowers its courts to issue them. Acknowledging the enormous noncompliance with Jewish law on this point, an amendment was added to the traditional *ketubah* stating that husband and wife agree to appear before a *bet din* at the other's request in case of civil divorce.

This amendment has not been widely used, and today some Conservative rabbis request that couples sign a separate prenuptial agreement in which both parties pledge that in case of civil divorce they will also terminate the marriage in accordance with Jewish law.

Prenuptial Agreement/*Tenaim*

In the event that the covenant of marriage entered into this ___ day of ___ 19 ___, by (husband) ___ and (wife) ___ shall be terminated or if they shall not have dwelled together for six consecutive months, then (husband) ___ and (wife) ___ shall voluntarily and promptly upon demand by either of the parties present themselves at a mutually convenient time and place to terminate the marriage and release each other from the covenant of marriage in accordance with Jewish law and custom.

This agreement is recognized as a material inducement to this marriage by the parties hereto. Failure of either of the parties to voluntarily perform his or her obligations hereunder if requested to do so by the other party shall render him or her liable for all costs, including attorneys' fees, reasonably incurred by the requesting party to secure his or her performance.

Entered into this ___ day of ___ 19 ___.

Signed by husband, wife, and two witnesses:

In the nineteenth century the Reform movement decided that civil divorce was fully valid and that no special Jewish recognition of the dissolution of a marriage was necessary. This decision was based largely upon the fact that the *get* ran counter to Reform's principle of complete equality in religious status for men and women. The vast majority of Reform rabbis thus will perform a second marriage without a *get*.

As the divorce rate among Jews has increased and rabbis do more and more marriage counseling, many Reform Jews have expressed a need for some kind of formal religious conclusion to marriages that were begun with Jewish ritual. So rabbis and couples have written new *gittim* and devised new divorce procedures.

The documents are generally reciprocal agreements in which both wife and husband pronounce their former partners free to remarry. While these procedures acknowledge the function and responsibility of the Jewish community in the dissolution of a marriage, they are not recognized as valid or binding by the Orthodox community.

In the *get* below two copies are written; one is given by the woman to the man, one by the man to the woman. The rabbi retains a third copy for his or her files. The text appears side by side in Hebrew and English.

REFORM *GET*

On the ___ day of the week, the ___ day of the month of ___ five thousand seven hundred ___ years since the creation of the world as we reckon here in ___ ___ located near ___ ___ daughter/son of ___ who resides in ___ said to ___ son/daughter of ___ I, of my own free will, grant you this bill of divorce. I hereby release you from the contract which established our marriage. From today onward, you are not my husband/wife and I am not your wife/husband. You belong to yourself and are free to marry any woman/man.

Signed by the woman, the man, two witnesses, and rabbi.[7]

This kind of *get* might be executed in a rabbi's study or synagogue sanctuary. If only one spouse is present for the ceremony, the document may be read and later delivered to the other. If both the man and woman are present, each brings a friend to act as witness and support. The ceremony can consist of just a few words from the rabbi and the reading of the divorce documents. The copy that remains on file with the rabbi might be cut or ripped as in Orthodox tradition, to physically enact the dissolution of the marriage covenant. The rabbi may pronounce the man and woman free to begin their new lives and marry whom they choose. While any formal acknowledgment of divorce is invariably painful, ceremonies such as these often provide a sense of resolution that might otherwise never occur.

For everything there is a season
and a time for every purpose under heaven:
A time to be born and a time to die,
a time to plant and a time to uproot . . .
a time for tearing down and a time for building up
a time for weeping and a time for laughing . . .
a time for embracing and a time to refrain from embracing.

APPENDICES

WEDDING POEMS

The voice of joy,
the voice of gladness,
the voice of the bridegroom,
the voice of the bride,
and the voice that praises God.

THE FIRST WEDDING IN THE WORLD

by Joel Rosenberg

I

The eighth day was the wedding.
He awoke amid a dewy moss,
and saw two swans gliding
between the cattails. It was dawn.

His side felt sore. He felt
a yearning where before
he'd felt protected, like a dream
had stolen out of reach.

It still was early,
and the moon still gleamed,

and crickets still posed
questions to their answering chorus.

Two large lions sat nearby,
amid the mist,
placidly gazing at the tiny rabbits
nibbling lettuce in their grassy niches.

II
The man had never seen an angel.
He thought it strange
that rainbow-colored fire
took on human image.

When he met Michael
and Gabriel, who told him
they were witnesses,
he thought their garments

were cascades of golden leaves,
their eyes a burning agate,
and their wings
a wreath of northern lights.

He called some names,
and beast and fowl
perked up their ears,
and forest noises filled the air.

III
God had the woman
waiting for him near the meadow,
standing on a shell,
her hair down to her knees.

She thought it all so strange,
this garden, jabbering animals,
this stranger standing dumbfounded
and stuttering out her name in joy.

She'd never seen a wedding canopy.
The golden gauze
was spun by angels
in the middle of the night.

She thought herself
a thousand years of age,
though looking like a girl of twenty,
all the sad, expensive wisdom

of society about to waken
in her bones, the secrets
of the wind and stars,
the human arts

of strife and cultivation,
tincture of the eyelids,
epic meters, and, as well,
concealments and apologies.

She smiled at the young man's
innocence, while, lovingly,
and for forever, she held out
her hand to him.

IV

The two of them,
with honeybees weaving among
the wreaths of flowers
at their brows,

the two of them,
with hope for clothes,
and no disqualifying memories,
and nothing that was not

within them from the start,
the two of them joined hands
and stood before the shimmering light
to make their vows.

June 19, 1977,
in honor of the wedding of Linda and William Novak
© Joel Rosenberg

THE SEVEN BLESSINGS

by Joel Rosenberg

Blessed is the One who plumps the grape
   and makes the vine a sapphire necklace
   curling through the humus of the vineyards
   in the summer dew,

and blessed is the One whose world is weighty
   like the crown of branches on the Tree of Life,

and blessed is the One who made the human being,
   fashioned in the hands from humus
   like a lump of clay,

and blessed is the One who gave the human,
   humus-born, the light of breath and speech,
   and made, from out of one, a two:
   a lasting structure, formed and shaped
   (who married all with joining words,
   enjoining all to know about the nakedness
   that may and may not be uncovered,
   and about the promised ones whose touch
   must be postponed, and gave forth unreservedly
   companionship beneath the canopy, with words
   across the cup of wine)!

Rejoice, rejoice, O devastated Lady!
   Let Jerusalem rejoice! and let her womb
   grow plump with children, gathered in
   from wandering in other worlds,
   like letters yearning to be speech,
   and blessed is the One
   who plants the fruit of joy
   inside the citadel
   atop her highest hill,

and dance and shout and sing, beloved friends,
   for in your laughter and your kisses
   is the blessed One, who gave us
   evanescent bliss in ancient days,
   inside the walled-in Garden

watered endlessly by springs and mists,
and blessed is that One who gives
a taste of Eden to the bridegroom and the bride,

and blessed is the One who fashioned songs
    and ululations, dervish spinnings, ecstasies,
    prophetic tongues, and jokes and puns,
    and double meanings and new teachings,
    and renewal of the Teaching,
    and the passion between lovers,
    and affection between friends and kin,
    and blessed is the One who gave us strength
    and peace!

        O quickly, quickly,
    Nameless One of ours, give Judah
    and the outskirts of Jerusalem
    the voice of weddings! Marry
    its inhabitants, and make us one
    with them, and make us One
    with You, and give us speech
    and poetry and pledges! Plump
    the grape for us to bless,
    and give us feasts and melodies,
    and make us drunk with You,
    O blessed One, who are
    both Bridegroom and a Bride!

July 1, 1979,
in honor of the wedding of Richard A. and Jeanne B. Siegel
© *Joel Rosenberg*

A SHEPHERD'S SONG IN MIDIAN

by Joel Rosenberg

I betroth you to me for an aeon,
I betroth you by the halo of the moon,
I bind to me, with you,
as I would bind a sign upon my hand,
the cricket antistrophes,
the rainbow and the quail.

I bind us by the fire on this mountain,
by the crackling thunder,
by the dancing alphabet above these rocks,
the sparking sage and bramble,
and the fleeing panther,
and the hind, poised, pausing
in her tracks.

Stand by me
in this yawning niche,
so recessed, like our vision,
yielding only outlines
of the past,

and I will place my shelter over you,
and, by the kernel of the pomegranate,
by the orange, and by the coriander,
by the henna of the lion's mane,
and by the oxen of the wood,
and by the learning of the elders,
and the merits of our mothers
Hannah, Sarah and Hagar,
and by the pain of Egypt,
and the steam of Goshen,
by the murmuring amid the tribes,
and by the shade of the tamar,

we'll tie aground the sky,
and open up the fountains in the granite,
and we'll split the seas like wineskins,
and we'll throw down history like a carpet
paved with snow and sapphire stones,
seen from afar.

And I will be a laborer for you,
and make the angels honor you,
and feed you words of manna,
and support you with a mighty hand.
And if I speak in stammers on your heart,
I'll speak to you with winning words,
and tell you: "Live, and flourish
like a sprouting of the field,"

and you shall know me, not
by names of mastery,
but you shall know me as your twin.

And I will bear you up on eagle's wings,
and I will guide you to a land
with skins of mists and dews,
her earth a garment for the body
of the dead,
and read to you the text of memory,
and tell you what was never said.

And I betroth you to me here,
correctly, even-temperedly,
but caring, and with tenderness.
My nurturing you'll know,
and I will be what I will be,
and you will be what you will be.
And who on earth has ever heard
about a union such as ours,
and who on earth has ever said
what we have said?

24 Tevet 5740 (January 13, 1980),
in honor of the wedding of Moshe Waldoks and Anne Pomerantz
© Joel Rosenberg

THE MYSTERY OF UNION

by Joel Rosenberg

As they, above, unite in one,
becoming One amid the mystery
of union, so, here below,

by call of ptarmigan and tern,
through summer cirrus feathers,
clove and fern, by symmetry

of witness, by the hand of scribe,
and ripening of time, we find
a place as one.

The hind
has panted for the stream.
The binding of the hand

has spelled the ancient themes
upon the heart. A gleam
of angels dances at the edges

of our words, while tablets
of our covenant
are hewn. A team of doves,

released like mist, the skirring
of their wings inscribe
a life's reunion with itself,

as you and I remember
how we stood together even then:
cicada, wind and thunder

growing dumb, the seaswells
hushed, Sambatyon
in pause. No lion roared,
no cattle lowed,
no horses neighed,
no peacocks crowed—

for one small instant
silence reigned, throughout
even the temples and the markets

of the Nile, while, slowly,
hardly louder than an aleph,
came the words: "I am"
and: "I am yours."

June 14, 1981,
in honor of the wedding of Les Bronstein and Benjy Schiller
© Joel Rosenberg

THE BRIDE ON JUBILEE

by Joel Rosenberg

The bride, discoursing
bashfully upon the Law,
invited anyone who listened
to come sit before her
and her bridegroom,
and obtain their blessing.
"Please don't be afraid."

Her words were spare.
The world had too much word
and information, anyway.
Her teachings fled like air,
though no words struck one
as being out of place.
They had a measured grace.

"The jubilee will be like this,"
she said, "the ram's horns
sounding, golden autumn sunshine
on the wheat. I think
that doves will also start
to gather in the land.
All teachings will taste sweet."

"Whatever happens," said
the groom, "the people will atone.
Changes of heart among those
harvesters, surprisingly,
can blossom almost anywhere,
even in fall—even October,
with a sadness in the air."

A congregant comes forward.
Trembling, he fumbles out
his patronymic. Sheltered
in the couple's woolen shawl,
he clasps their hands.
Smiling, they give him all
that's in their power to confer.

Their prayer text, moist
as the seeds of a late planting,
scatters like the skirr of pigeons
flushed out by the snappings
of the fruit grown heavy
on the twig. Words enter,
dark, disguised, engendering,

into earth, worn smooth
by use. The moon, newborn,
has doused their dew with silver
crescents. Breaking
like the glass beneath
a bridegroom's foot, they breed,
fruitful and multiplying.

May 1979,
In honor of the wedding of Ina Elfant and Steven Asher
© Joel Rosenberg

THE SUCCAH AND THE HUPPAH

by Debra Cash

We live in the world; most of us live in houses and apartment buildings, near busy streets. But there are two temporary structures that we build in our life-times. One is the succah, the desert booth. The other is the huppah, the wedding canopy.

Every year, the succah reminds us that once we had no permanent place, no land where we could sow and expect to reap at the end of a long growing season. It reminds us that once we were wanderers in the wilder-ness, and we longed for a home. We talk about how easily the succah collapses. It has firm walls, so that we can almost pretend that it is real, but we lay tree branches across the roof for thatch, tie paper birds and gourds from the rafters, and count the stars through the leaves.

The huppah is different. Who could mistake it for a real house? Its walls are nonexistent. The roof is flimsy.

Wind can blow through the huppah. The rain is welcome. The couple who stand under its shelter must leave it to look up and see the stars.

But it is the huppah that we take for our home when we are promising each other everything. It is raised, for most of us, once in a lifetime. It is not permanent. But it is the promise of a home.

Its openness pledges that there will be no secrets. Friends and family stand at the corners, weighing the fragile structure down. The roof is often a tallit so that the bride and groom are covered by holiness and the memory of commandments.

The huppah does not promise that love or hope or pledges will keep out weather or catastrophe. But its few lines are a sketch for what might be.

The man and woman have left the desert of their loneliness. They have come from far away to be together. The flimsiness of the huppah reminds them that the only thing that is real about a home is the people in it who love and choose to be together, to be a family. The only anchor that they will have will be holding onto each others' hands.

The huppah is the house of promises. It is the home of hope.

15 Sivan 5742/June 6, 1982,
for the sheva b'rachot *of Yehuda Bodenstein Avniel and Sara Reva Horowitz*
© 1982, Debra Cash

ESHET CHAYIL
A NEW VERSION

by Susan Grossman

A good wife who can find her
she is worth far more than rubies
she brings good and not harm

all the days of her life
she girds herself with strength
and finds her trades profitable
wise counsel is on her tongue
and her home never suffers for warmth
she stretches her hands to the poor
reaches her arms to the needy
all her friends praise her
her family blesses her
she is known at the gates
as she sits with the elders
dignity, honor are her garb
she smiles at the future.

A good man who can find him
he is worth far more than rubies
all who trust in him
never lack for gain
he shares the household duties
and sets a goodly example
he seeks a satisfying job
and braces his arms for work
he opens his mouth with wisdom
he speaks with love and kindness
his justice brings him praises
he raises the poor, lowers the haughty.

These two indeed do worthily
true leaders in Zion
give them their due credit
let their words praise them at the gates.

THE CHUPPAH

by Marge Piercy

The chuppah stands on four poles.
The home has four corners.
The chuppah stands on four poles.

The marriage stands on four legs.
Four points loose the winds
that blow on the walls of the house,
the south wind that brings the warm rain,
the east wind that brings the cold rain,
the north wind that brings the cold sun
and the snow, the long west wind
bringing the weather off the far plains.

Here we live open to the seasons.
Here the winds caress and cuff us
contrary and fierce as bears.
Here the winds are caught and snarling
in the pines, a cat in a net clawing
breaking twigs to fight loose.
Here the winds brush your face
soft in the morning as feathers
that float down from the dove's breast.

Here the moon sails up out of the ocean
dripping like a just washed apple.
Here the sun wakes us like a baby.
Therefore the chuppah has no sides.

It is not a box.
It is not a coffin.
It is not a dead end.
Therefore the chuppah has no walls
We have made a home together
open to the weather of our time.
We are mills that turn in the winds of struggle
converting fierce energy into bread.

The canopy is the cloth of our table
where we share fruit and vegetables
of our labor, where our care for the earth
comes back and we take its body in ours.

The canopy is the cover of our bed
where our bodies open their portals wide,
where we eat and drink the blood
of our love, where the skin shines red

as a swallowed sunrise and we burn
in one furnace of joy molten as steel
and the dream is flesh and flower.

O my love O my love we dance
under the chuppah standing over us
like an animal on its four legs,
like a table on which we set our love
as a feast, like a tent
under which we work
not safe but no longer solitary
in the searing heat of our time.

June 2, 1982,
on her marriage to Ira Wood
© *1982, Marge Piercy*

WE COME TOGETHER

by Ira Wood

WE come together
Pure and ample
Top heavy woman
Stocky man
Midwestern half breed
Long Island Jew.

Jew with eyes like jade
Jew with eyes like almonds
Jews with tempers
Like the blue serpent tongue
of the lightning that cracks
the sky over our land.

WE come together strong
Strong as our passion to lay
skin pressed to skin, quivering,
strong as our hunger
to tell, to taste, to know.

I am lucky to have you
I know it.

But with each windfall
comes the tax
With each rainfall
the weeds
To kneel and pull.

WE give and take
with no line between
WE grow our food
WE heal our wounds.
You remind me
Good writing takes time,
I bolster you
When the world attacks.

WE came together
each an other.
WE come together now
sister brother
mother son
father daughter
man and woman
each bond in its turn.
WE lick each other's skins like lost kittens
Fight like hungry strays
WE will talk deep into the night
Make each other coffee
Keep each other straight.

WE are scrub oak
Strong and low
Peony
Full bodies, brilliant
Feast for the butterfly
Feast for the ant.

Our love is like the land.
WE work it to keep it fertile.

June 2, 1982,
on his marriage to Marge Piercy
© *1984, Ira Wood*

FOUR TRANSLATIONS
FROM THE SONG OF SONGS:
Love Poems from the Bible

by Marcia Falk

VII

In sandy earth or deep
In valley soil
I grow, a wildflower thriving
On your love.

Narcissus in the brambles,
Brightest flower—
I choose you from all others
For my love.

Sweet fruit tree growing wild
Within the thickets—
I blossom in your shade
And taste your love.

IX

The sound of my lover
coming from the hills
quickly, like a deer
upon the mountains

Now at my windows,
walking by the walls,
here at the lattices
he calls—

Come with me,
my love,
come away

For the long wet months are past,
the rains have fed the earth
and left it bright with blossoms

Birds wing in the low sky,
dove and songbird singing
in the open air above

Earth nourishing tree and wine,
green fig and tender grape,
green and tender fragrance

Come with me,
my love,
come away

XVIII

Enclosed and hidden, you are a garden,
A still pool, a fountain.

Stretching your limbs, you open—
A field of pomegranates blooms,

Treasured fruit among the blossoms,
Henna, sweet cane, bark, and saffron,

Fragrant woods and succulents,
The finest spices and perfumes.

Living water, you are a fountain,
A well, a river flowing from the mountains.

Come, north winds and south winds!
Breathe upon my garden,

Bear its fragrance to my lover,
Let him come and share its treasures.

My bride, my sister, I have come
To gather spices in my garden,

To taste wild honey with my wine,
Milk and honey with my wine.

FEAST, DRINK—AND DRINK DEEPLY—LOVERS!

XXVIII

Stamp me in your heart,
Upon your limbs,

Sear my emblem deep
Into your skin.

For love is strong as death,
Harsh as the grave.
Its tongues are flames, a fierce
And holy blaze.

Endless seas and floods,
Torrents and rivers
Never put out love's
Infinite fires.

Those who think that wealth
Can buy them love
Only play the fool
And meet with scorn.

© *Marcia Lee Falk, 1973, 1977*

According to the translator, three different voices speak these poems: singular male, singular female, and a group of speakers. These are distinguishable in the original because Hebrew declensions reflect gender. Thus the lines of roman (nonitalicized) type correspond to the male speaker, the female voice is italicized, and the passage spoken by a group appears capitalized.

THE CHILDREN
OF NOAH:
A
WEDDING CEREMONY

By Rebecca Alpert, Linda Holtzman,
and Arthur Waskow*

___

1. If at all possible, the setting and symbols of the ceremony should reflect the motif of the Rainbow Covenant, that not only the whole human race but all forms of life are in covenant with God. For instance, the wedding might be held outdoors. If this is impossible, greenery and living plants might surround the setting. Over the area where the ceremony takes place, there might be a bow-shaped arch painted like a rainbow or perhaps a lattice covered with flowers. Some participants might hold clusters of flowers or balloons in the colors of the rainbow.

2. In full sight of the congregation, begin by pouring or sprinkling from a pitcher of water a circle on the earth or floor where the ceremony is to take place—and then within this circle, a circle of sand. The water represents the Flood,

___

* Alpert is a rabbi and dean of students at the Reconstructionist Rabbinical College, Holtzman is a congregational rabbi in Coatesville, PA, and Waskow is the editor of *Menorah* and a member of the RRC faculty. This ceremony first appeared in the November/December 1983 issue of *Menorah: Sparks of Jewish Renewal*, a publication by A Center for Jewish Renewal of the Public Resource Center, in Philadelphia, PA. It was published with a detailed discussion of the symbolism of the rainbow and the place of this ceremony in Jewish life.

the sand that earthen boundary of dry land that God raised up against the Flood. The wedding takes place within the inner circle.

3. The couple comes forward, separately, with whatever companions they wish. The two of them enter the inner circle; others stand just outside it.

4. The couple sings or recites from the Song of Songs (together or in dialogue with each other):

> *Come, love, let us go out into the open fields*
> *And spend our night lying where the henna blooms,*
> *Rising early to leave for the near vineyard*
> *Where the vines flower, opening tender buds,*
> *And the pomegranate boughs unfold their blossoms.*
> *There among blossom and vine will I give you my love.*
>
> *Stamp me in your heart,*
> *Upon your limbs.*
> *Sear my emblem deep*
> *Into your skin.*
>
> *For love is strong as death*
> *Harsh as the grave.*
> *Its tongues are flames,*
> *A fierce and holy blaze.**

5. A "chain" of seven knotted-together scarves of the seven colors of the rainbow is draped over the couple's shoulders. They say to each other:

> *I join in covenant with you and God and every living creature,*
> *In the sign of the Bow that appears in the clouds,*
> *That together we shall so act*
> *That seedtime and harvest,*
> *Cold and heat,*
> *Summer and winter,*
> *Day and night*
> *Shall not cease;*
> *That between the Jewish people and the other peoples,*

---

* Translation by Marcia Falk ©.

Between our peoples and among all peoples,
We shall banish bow, sword, and battle from the earth.

And I join in covenant with you and God
That through all changes
In the weather of our lives—
In seedtime and harvest,
In cold and heat,
In suffering and joy—
I will share with you my body, my feelings, my thoughts, my
spirit;
I will make Torah present in our lives together.

6. After slipping a ring onto the other's finger each one says to the other:

> *With this ring*
> *I espouse you to me.*
> *I espouse you in righteousness and justice,*
> *In goodness and loving kindness.*
> *I espouse you in faithfulness.*

7. The facilitator of the ceremony reads aloud a written statement as follows:

On the ___ day of the month of ___ in the year ___ according to the common reckoning, and in the year ___ since the Creation of the World, ___ and ___, children of Adam and Chava, Noah and Naamah, said to each other in the presence of witnesses:
(Repeat the pledge in 6 above.)

And they further made a covenant that read (Read whatever else the couple agrees to. This may be a document that is witnessed and signed.)

8. The couple says aloud (or the facilitator can put these in the form of questions to which they answer "We will" or "We do"):
Together we shall share the four elements of fire, water, earth, and air—as a sign that we now share our lives together.

We pledge ourselves to light this fire not to burn the earth and destroy all life, but to make a light with which we can see God's Image clearly, in each other and all life. (Light candles.)

We pledge ourselves to share God's bounty from the earth with each other and the hungry of the earth. (Share grapes or other food.)

We pledge ourselves not to flood ourselves and drown the world in danger, but to sustain each other as we drink. (Each pours a glass of water for the other and both drink.)

(They turn to face the congregation and say:) We are prepared to share God's gift of air from the Breath of Life.

9. Congregants may join with the facilitator in saying:

> *By the authority vested in us*
> *Through the covenant of God with all of Noah's children,*
> *Through the teachings of the Torah,*
> *And through the laws of the State of* ___
> *We proclaim you husband and wife*
> *(or "spouses" or "life partners"*
> *or any other formulation)*

10. The couple say aloud, together: We pledge ourselves to share the Breath of Life. (Kiss.)

11. Participants shout *Mazel Tov*. At this point they could also toss their multi-colored flowers or release set of balloons to drift off into the sky.

TRADITIONAL TENAIM TEXT

To a Good Fortune

May it come up and sprout forth like a green garden
whoso finds a wife finds a great good, and obtains
favor of the good Lord who ratifies this union

May He who predestinates, bestow a good name and future to the provisions embodied in this agreement, which were agreed upon by the two parties hereto, that is, as party of the first part, Mr. ____ who represents the groom, Mr. ____, and as party of the second part, Mr. ____ who represents the bride Miss ____.

Firstly: That the above named groom agrees to take himself as wife the above named bride, through *huppah* and betrothal, in accordance with the Laws of Moses and Israel; that they will neither abstract nor conceal from one another any property whatsoever, but they shall equally have power over their property, pursuant to the established custom.

The above named groom obligates himself to present the bride with gifts according to custom.

The above named bride obligates herself to give as her dowry the sum of ____ in cash, and clothes, pillows and linens, as is the custom.

The wedding will take place, if the Almighty so

wills it, on the ___ day of ___ in the year ___ or sooner than such date if both parties agree thereto.

A find is to be paid, by the party breaking this agreement, to the other party, in the fixed sum of ___ and also in accordance with the laws of the land.

All of the forgoing was done with perfect understanding and due deliberation, and by means of the most effective method, in accordance with the ordinances of the sages, of blessed memory, and in accordance with the laws of the land; by means of striking hands, by solemn promises, by true affirmation, by handing over an object (from one contracting party to another), to take effect immediately; and this is not to be regarded as a mere forfeiture without consideration, or as a mere formula or document. We have followed the legal formality of a symbolic delivery *(kinyan)*, by handing over an object, between the groom and the bride and their representatives, by using a garment legally fit for the purpose, to validate all that is stated above.

AND EVERYTHING IS VALID AND CONFIRMED

Attested to _____ groom
Attested to _____ bride

Attested to _____ witness
Attested to _____ witness

DIRECTORY OF ARTISTS

The widespread and burgeoning revival of Jewish arts in the United States makes a comprehensive listing impossible. What follows is an altogether idiosyncratic list of artists whose work is known to me, some of whose creations appear in this book.

Frann Addison
100 Cypress Street
Watertown, MA 02172
(pewter and glass)

Rose Ann Chasman
6147 North Richmond
Chicago, IL 60659
(calligraphy, paper cuts)

Leslie Gattmann and
Eugene Frank
7410 Poplar Drive
Forestville, CA 95436
(porcelain, ceramics)

Shonna Husbands-Hankin
36351 Government Road
Dorena, OR 97434
(calligraphy)

Phyllis Kantor
250 East 38 Avenue
Eugene, OR 97405
(weaving)

Miriam Karp
880 Somerset Drive NW
Atlanta, GA 30327
(calligraphy, graphics)

Elee Koplow
134 Wallis Road
Chestnut Hill, MA 02167
(ceramic artist; sculpture
and murals)

Jonathan Kremer
219 Hastings Avenue
Havertown, PA 19083
(calligraphy)

Susan Leviton .
3417 North 4th Street
Harrisburg, PA 17110
(calligraphy)

Claire Mendelson
499 Fort Washington
   Avenue, 6-H
New York, NY 10033
(calligraphy)

Philip Ritari
113 College Avenue
Somerville, MA 02144
(calligraphy)

Lesley Rubin
35 Coolidge Hill Road
Watertown, MA 02172
(calligraphy, graphics)

Batya Silverman
P. O. Box 3172
Beverly Hills, CA 90212
(calligraphy)

Elly Simmons
P.O. Box 463
Lagunitas, CA 94938
(calligraphy)

Betsy Platkin Teutsch
789 West End Avenue, 9-C
New York, NY 10025
(calligraphy)

Tsirl Waletzky
80 Knolls Crescent
Bronx, NY 10463
(papercuts; needlework
design)

POETS

Debra Cash, a former executive editor of *genesis 2*, is a journalist and poet who lives in Watertown, Massachusetts.

Marcia Falk is a poet and translator who teaches literature at the University of Judaism in Los Angeles. Her translation of Song of Songs is currently out of print, but copies are available from the author for $9.50 each. Send to:

> Marcia Falk
> c/o University of Judaism
> 15600 Mulholland Drive
> Los Angeles, CA 90077

Susan Grossman is a poet who lives in Brooklyn, New York. A rabbinical student at the Jewish Theological Seminary, she writes and lectures about Jewish women. Her essays have appeared in *The Jewish Spectator*, *The Long Island Jewish World*, and also in *Jewish and Female* (Susan Schneider, ed. New York, Simon & Schuster, 1984)

Marge Piercy is a novelist, poet, essayist, reviewer, and teacher. Her most recent book of poems is *Stone, Paper, Knife* (New York, Knopf, 1983)

Joel Rosenberg is Associate Professor of Hebrew Literature and Judaic Studies at Tufts University. His articles, essays, and poems have appeared in *Response*, *Moment*, *Midstream*, and *National Jewish Monthly*, among other publications. His book on political allegory and the Bible is forthcoming from Crossroads Press.

Ira Wood is a fiction writer and playwright.

NOTES

Introduction

1 Rabbi Harold Schulweis, "Blessed Are Our Differences," *Moment Magazine*, Vol. 8, No. 8 (Sept. 1983/Tishrei 5744).

PART ONE: MAKING THE TRADITION YOUR OWN

The Tradition of Marriage

1 Rabbi Maurice Lamm, *The Jewish Way in Love and Marriage* (San Francisco: Harper & Row, 1980), pp. 128-129 (Yevamot 63b).

2 Philip and Hanna Goodman, *The Jewish Marriage Anthology* (Philadelphia: Jewish Publication Society of America, 1965), p. 44 (Zohar 1:89a).

3 Lawrence Kushner, *The River of Light, Spirituality, Judaism and the Evolution of Consciousness* (San Francisco: Harper & Row, 1981), p. xii.

4 My adaptation of the story from *Pirke de Rabbi Eliezer*, trans. Gerald Friedlander (New York: Sepher-Hermon Press), p. 88, and Goodman, p. 34.

5 Goodman, p. 24 (Babylonian Talmud, Sotah 2a).

6 Goodman, p. 37 (Genesis Rabba, 68:4).

7 Lamm, p. 119.

8 Goodman, p. 30 (Baba Metzia 59a).

9 Ibid., p. 27 (Kiddushin 29b-30a).

Modern Options

10 For a sampling of the current discussion on women and Halakhah, see: Blu Greenberg, *On Women and Judaism: The*

View from Tradition (Philadelphia: Jewish Publication Society, 1981); Susannah Heschel, ed. *On Being a Jewish Feminist* (New York: Schocken Books, 1983); Elizabeth Koltun, ed. *The Jewish Woman* (New York: Schocken Books, 1976); Susan Schneider, ed. *Jewish and Female* (New York: Simon & Schuster, 1984).

How Jewish a Wedding Do You Want?

11 An interesting discussion of family conflict is found in Rabbi Edwin H. Friedman's article, "Systems and Ceremonies: A Family View of Rites of Passage," from *The Family Life Cycle: A Framework for Family Therapy*, Monica McGoldrick and Elizabeth Carter, eds. (New York: Gardiner Press, 1980) pp. 429–452.

Anticipating Conflict

12 Friedman, "Systems and Ceremonies."

When Jews Marry Non-Jews

13 I discussed the subject of intermarriage with virtually everyone I encountered in the course of researching this book. In particular I'd like to thank Rabbi Al Axelrad, Debra Cash, Rabbi Everett Gendler, Rabbi Lawrence Kushner, Drora Setel, Rabbi Daniel Shevitz, Rabbi Max Ticktin, and Arthur Waskow.

14 Helen Latner, *The Book of Modern Jewish Etiquette* (New York: Schocken Books, 1981), p. 208.

PART TWO: WAYS AND MEANS

Information in this section came from conversations with the following: Lev Friedman, Rabbi Stuart Geller, Rabbi Lawrence Kushner, Reb Zalman Schachter-Shalomi, Rabbi Daniel Shevitz, Rabbi Jeffrey Summit, Rabbi Max Ticktin, Rabbi Rebecca Trachtenberg Alpert.

Choosing a Rabbi

1 Rabbi Maurice Lamm, *The Jewish Way in Love and Marriage* (San Francisco: Harper & Row, 1981), p. 179.

When and Where

2 Abraham Joshua Heschel, *The Sabbath: Its Meaning for Modern Man* (New York: Farrar, Straus & Giroux, 1981), p. 8.
3 Ibid.
4 Philip and Hanna Goodman, *The Jewish Marriage Anthology* (Philadelphia: Jewish Publication Society of America, 1965), p. 172.

Wedding Clothes, Wedding Rings

5 Richard Siegel, Sharon Strassfeld, and Michael Strassfeld, *The First Jewish Catalog* (Philadelphia: Jewish Publication Society, 1973), p. 57.
6 Lamm, p. 221.
7 Lamm, p. 222.
8 For information about jewelers, see *The First Jewish Catalog* and *The New Jewish Yellow Pages* by Mae Shafter Rockland (Englewood, N.J.: SBS Publishing, Inc., 1980).

The Ketubah

9 "The *ketubah* did bond us in a special way in that it helped us to clarify our Jewish values and human values as individuals and as a couple. We realized that although we use different vocabulary when describing our feelings about marriage, commitment, and family, we are actually saying the same thing. In writing the *ketubah*, the vocabulary became the same for both of us, and this enabled us to see even more clearly why it is that we chose to become part of the Jewish community as husband and wife" (from a letter written by Joni-Sue Blinderman of Brookline, Massachusetts).
10 Lamm, p. 198.
11 Goodman, p. 90.
12 Ibid.
13 Moses Gaster, *The Ketubah* (publ. 1924; rptd New York: Sepher-Hermon Press, 1974), p. 48.
14 Ibid., p. 20.
15 I heard the words *brit ketubah* from Rabbi Max Ticktin of Washington, D.C., whose knowledge informs much of this chapter.
16 Resources on Hebrew calligraphy: *The First Jewish Catalog*,

pp. 184-209; Ludwig F. Toby, *The Art of Hebrew Lettering* (Tel Aviv: Schuster Publishers, 1973).

17 Zalman Schachter-Shalomi with Donald Gropman, *The First Step* (New York: Bantam Books, 1983), p. 40.

18 This is also commonly known as the "*Jewish Catalog* Ketubah," where it appeared in 1973.

19 This *ketubah* text, illustrated in color and calligraphed in both Hebrew and English by Wendy Rebecca Friedman, has been reproduced and is available. For information, write: Ketubot, 14 Chatham Circle, Brookline, MA 02146.

The Huppah

20 Goodman, p. 97.

21 Rabbi Aryeh Kaplan, *Made in Heaven* (New York: Moznaim Publishing Co., 1983), p. 145.

22 Ellen Deutch Quint, "Huppah Whoopee," *The Jewish Women's Resource Center Newsletter*, Vol. II, No. 2, Fall 1980, pp. 8–9. National Council of Jewish Women, New York Section.

The Processional

23 Goodman, p. 28.

24 Hayyim Schauss, *The Lifetime of a Jew* (New York: Union of American Hebrew Congregations, 1950), pp. 187–88.

25 Rabbi Lawrence Kushner.

26 Write for catalogs to the following, which are good sources for music:

> Transcontinental Music Publications
> 838 Fifth Avenue
> New York, NY 10021
> (sheet music for voices, organ, piano,
> and other instruments)

> Tara Publications
> 29 Derby Avenue
> Cedarhurst, NY 11516
> (especially for songbooks)

For Israeli songs, including many from Shir haShirim, see *Israel in Song* and *Great Songs of Israel*.

27 Rabbi Burt Jacobson, "Jewish Wedding Workbook," p. 60.

28 Lamm, p. 214.

29 Kaplan, *Made in Heaven*, p. 161. The seven relatives that become forbidden to the groom are: the bride's mother, her daughter, her sister, her mother's mother, her father's mother, her son's daughter, and her daughter's daughter.

30 By Linda Hirschhorn © 1983. From the wedding ceremony of Linda Hirschhorn and David Cooper. In their wedding ceremony the circling was done after the seven marriage blessings, immediately before the breaking of the glass.

31 See n. 26, above.

Witnesses

32 Samson Raphael Hirsch, *Horeb* (London: Soncino Press, 1973), p. 533.

33 Lamm, p. 168.

Food and Drink

34 Samuel H. Dresner, *The Jewish Dietary Laws* (New York: Burning Bush Press, 1955), p. 19.

35 For more information about *kashrut*, see: *The Jewish Dietary Laws*, ibid.; *The First Jewish Catalog*, pp. 18–36; Rabbi Hayim Halevy Donin, *To Be a Jew* (New York: Basic Books, 1972), pp. 97–120.

36 A felicitous formulation by Rabbi Eugene Borowitz.

37 Thanks to Miss Pattie Chase (my caterer, my friend) for her helpful comments on the selection and handling of caterers.

Laughter, Music, and Dance

Thanks to Moshe Waldoks, whose knowledge and wit inform this discussion of *badchanut*. Rikki Lippitz' and Joshua Jacobson's musical expertise informs this chapter's discussion of wedding music.

38 Goodman, pp. 105–111.

39 Schauss, p. 186.

40 Sources for sheet music and songbooks are listed above in n. 26 in the section "The Processional." For Yiddish folk songs, see Tara Publications' *Mir Trogen a Gesang: The New Book of Yiddish Song*, with transliterations and historical background as well as guitar chords.

41 Hayyim Schneid, *Marriage* (Jerusalem: Keter Books, 1973) p. 42–43.

Photographers and Flowers

Thanks to my friend and my photographer Peggy McMahon for her comments, which inform this section.

PART THREE: CELEBRATIONS AND RITUALS

Tenaim: *Celebrating Engagement*

1 Samson Raphael Hirsch, *Horeb* (London: Soncino Press, 1962), p. 533.

2 This is a description of the *tenaim* ceremony by and for Barbara Rosman Penzner and Brian Penzner Rosman. Copies of the entire ceremony may be obtained for the cost of copying and postage from the Creative Liturgy Library of the Reconstructionist Rabbinical College, Church Road and Greenwood Avenue, Wyncote, PA 19095.

When I met Barbara Rosman Penzner she was both a student at the Reconstructionist Rabbinical College and a bride. She was an invaluable resource and inspiration for this chapter and much of this book.

Celebrating Community

3 Barbara Rosner Penzner and Brian Penzner Rosner wrote these words originally for the celebration of their *tenaim*.

4 For more information and ideas about making *tallesim* and other gifts, see *The First Jewish Catalog* (Philadelphia: Jewish Publication Society, 1973), and *The New Jewish Yellow Pages* (Englewood, N.J.: SBS Publishing Inc., 1980).

5 The Mi She'beirakh is so called for the first words of the prayer, which are traditionally translated, "He who blessed our fathers, Abraham, Isaac and Jacob, may He bless . . ." This is a "prayer for all occasions," according to Rabbi Hayim Halevy Donin, *To Pray as a Jew* (New York: Basic Books, 1980), p. 251. It may be said on behalf of a sick person or to wish well to a bar mitzvah or for the health of a newborn child and its mother. It is also the setting for naming girl children in the synagogue. The Mi She'beirakh on

behalf of a couple about to be married invokes God's blessing on the bride and groom, with wishes for their happiness and success in creating a Jewish home. In some congregations the opening lines of this prayer have been modified to read: "God who blessed our fathers and mothers, Abraham and Sarah, Isaac and Rebecca, Jacob and Leah and Rachel, may God bless . . ."

Spiritual Preparation

Thanks to Penina Adelman, Rabbi Burt Jacobson, Cherie Kohler-Fox, Barbara Rosman Penzner, Zalman Schachter-Shalomi, Drorah Setel, Moshe Waldoks, Arthur Waskow.

6 For a thoughtful examination of *mikvah* and the laws of *taharat hamishpacha* see the essay by Rachel Adler in *The Jewish Woman*, ed. Elizabeth Koltun (New York: Schocken Books, 1976).

7 Since biblical times Jews have immersed themselves in *mikvaot* in order to transform *tumah* into *taharah*, terms generally translated, respectively, as "unclean" and "pure." However, some people believe that this translation has led to a misunderstanding of the meaning of *mikvah*.

When the Temple stood in Jerusalem, the High Priest entered the Holy of Holies only once a year, on Yom Kippur. When he emerged from the innermost sanctuary he had to immerse himself in a *mikvah* before putting on his robes. Clearly, this encounter with the holy did not make him "unclean"; however, in coming so close to the Source of power, he became *tamay*. The preparation of corpses for burial, which is considered a great *mitzvah*, also renders one *tamay;* so does childbirth.

Although the Bible implies that the cycle of *tumah/taharah* was a way for everyone to experience the terrifying/mysterious/holy processes of death and rebirth, after the destruction of the Temple, most of the laws of *tumah* that applied to men were discarded. The laws regarding *niddah* became codified into *taharat hamishpacha* (the purity of the family), and, as Rachel Adler writes in *The Jewish Woman*, *tamay* "became a special condition afflicting only women."

8 Rabbi Aryeh Kaplan, *Waters of Eden: The Mystery of the Mikvah* (New York: National Conference of Synagogue Youth/ Union of Orthodox Jewish Congregations, 1976), p. 35.

9 Thanks to Penina Adelman, whose article "Nisan: Time to Redig Miriam's Well" (*genesis 2*, March-April 1983/Nisan 5743) is the source for this ceremony.

10 Richard Siegel and Carl Rheins, eds. *The Jewish Almanac* (New York: Bantam Books, 1980), pp. 541–542.

11 These prayers come from a *mikvah* celebration entitled "The Voice of God Echoes Across the Waters," which may be obtained for the cost of copying and postage from the Creative Liturgy Library of the Reconstructionist Rabbinical College, Church Road and Greenwood Avenue, Wyncote, PA 19095.

12 This poem, written by Gerald Dicker, appears in *Vehater Libeynu* (Purify Our Hearts) *siddur* of Congregation Beth El of the Sudbury River Valley, Sudbury, MA (1980), p. 114.

13 From "A Jewish Wedding Workbook," by Rabbi Burt Jacobson.

The Wedding Day

Thanks are due Barbara Rosman Penzner, Penina Adelman, Nina Beth Cardin (who assisted me with the files of the Jewish Women's Resource Center, National Council of Jewish Women, New York Section), Lev Freidman, Rabbi Jeff Summit, Reb Zalman Schachter-Shalomi, and Moshe Waldoks.

Betrothal: The Ring Ceremony

14 Rabbi Maurice Lamm, *The Jewish Way in Love and Marriage* (San Francisco: Harper & Row, 1981), also see Kaplan, *Made in Heaven* p. 135.

15 Translation by Debra Cash.

16 From a wedding booklet written by Rabbi William Feyer, Atlanta, Georgia.

17 From a wedding service written by Rabbi Burt Jacobson.

18 Rabbi Wolli Kaelter of Long Beach, CA. Privately printed and distributed.

19 The common addition of "as my wife" (and also "as my husband") in the English translation of the *haray aht* reflects the differentiation of gender apparent in Hebrew nouns.

20 Rabbi Aryeh Kaplan, *Made in Heaven* (New York: Moznaim Publishing Co., 1983), p. 177.

Nuptials: The Seven Marriage Blessings

21 Many of these comments about the *sheva b'rachot* are paraphrased from a conversation with Rabbi Avram Aryan, to whom I am indebted for his comments about history, creation, and redemption in the marriage blessings.

22 From a conversation with Rabbi Zalman Schachter-Shalomi.

Finales

23 The Talmud was finally edited no later than the fifth century, C.E.

24 Goodman, p. 28.

25 Lamm, p. 229.

26 Daniel I. Leifer, "On Writing New Ketubot," *The Jewish Woman*, Elizabeth Koltun, ed. (New York: Schocken Books, 1976) pp. 50–61.

Blessings for the Simcha

27 Sheila Peltz Weinberg, "Kashrut: How Do We Eat?," *The Jewish Family Book* eds. Sharon Strassfeld and Kathy Green (Toronto: Bantam Books, 1981), p. 86.

28 Information regarding *sheva shevahot* comes from the files of the Jewish Women's Resource Center, NCJW, 9 East 69 Street, New York, NY 10021. Particularly useful were the two *sheva shevahot* ceremonies compiled by Serena Wieder and Beverly Worthman. Winter 1978.

29 This translation of *birkat hamazon* is adapted from *Vetaher Libeynu* (Purify Our Hearts), the *siddur* of Congregation Beth El of the Sudbury River Valley. Other sources include a translation by Rabbi Zalman Schachter-Shalomi, and the discussion of *birkat hamazon* in Donin, *To Pray as a Jew*, pp. 287–301.

PART FOUR: HUSBANDS AND WIVES

A Jewish Home

1 *Vetaher Libeynu* (Purify Our Hearts), *siddur* of Congregation Beth El of the Sudbury River Valley, Sudbury, MA (1980), p. 8.

2   From a poem by Debra Cash that appears on pages 230–31.
3   From the *ketubah* by Rabbi Gustav Buchdahl, Rabbi Law-
     rence Kushner, and Rabbi Bernard H. Mehlman that ap-
     pears in full on pages 90–91.

   Divorce

4   Gittin 90b.
5   National resources include:

       Beth Din of America
          (Orthodox)
       1250 Broadway
       New York, NY 10010

       G.E.T.
          (Getting Equitable Treatment:
          an organization that seeks to
          expedite Jewish divorce law)
       P.O. Box 131
       Brooklyn, NY 11230

6   Bracha Osofsky, "Progress on the Get Problem," *Lilith*, No.
     10 (Winter 1982–83), pp. 4–5.
7   Text by Rabbis Harold Bloom and Lawrence Kushner.

GLOSSARY

AGUNAH Literally, "a chained woman": one whose marriage has not been terminated according to Jewish law and who is thus prohibited from remarrying

ALEPH-BET Name of the Hebrew alphabet; also, its first two letters

ALIYAH Literally, "to go up": to be called to the Torah. Also, "making *aliyah*" refers to moving to the land of Israel.

ARAMAIC Semitic language closely related to Hebrew, the lingua franca of the Middle East. The Talmud was written in Aramaic, as are traditional legal documents, including *ketubah*, *tenaim*, and *get*.

ASHKENAZIC Jews and Jewish culture of Eastern and Central Europe

AUFRUF Recognition of a groom (and bride) by calling them up to the Torah on the Shabbat immediately preceding a wedding

BAAL SHEM TOV Israel ben Eliezer, founder of Hasidism, the eighteenth-century mystical revival movement

BADCHAN Master of ceremonies at a wedding celebration

BARUCH ATA ADONAI Words that begin Hebrew blessings, most commonly rendered in English as "Blessed art Thou, Lord our God." (This book contains many alternatives to that translation.)

B.C.E. Before the Common Era. (Jews avoid using the Christian designation B.C., which means "before Christ.")

BEDEKEN Ritual ceremony of veiling the bride before the wedding ceremony

BET DIN   Rabbinical court

BIMAH   Raised platform in the synagogue

BRIS/BRIT   Covenant. *Bris* and *brit milah* refer to the covenant of circumcision.

C.E.   Common Era. (Jews avoid the designation A.D., which means "in the year of our Lord.")

CHALLAH   Braided loaf of white bread, traditional for Shabbat and the holidays

CHOSSEN   Yiddish for "groom"; in Hebrew, *hatan*

CHOSSEN'S TISH   Literally, "groom's table": the name of the celebration for the groom and his friends prior to the wedding ceremony

CONSERVATIVE   Religious movement, developed in the United States during the twentieth century as a more traditional response to modernity than that offered by Reform

DAVEN   Pray

D'RASH   Religious insight, often on a text from the Torah

D'VAR TORAH   Literally, "words of Torah": an explication about a portion of the Torah

ERUSIN   Betrothal ceremony

FLAYSHIG   Meat food, which, according to *kashrut*, may not be mixed with dairy products

FREILACH   Yiddish for "happy"; also, up-tempo songs

GET   Formal document of Jewish divorce

HALAKHAH   Jewish law of the Talmud

HASIDISM   Eighteenth-century mystical revival movement that stressed God's immanence in the world. The doctrine of *simcha*, joy, was expounded as a way of communing with God; *simcha* was expressed in singing, dancing, feasting, and rejoicing.

HATAN   Hebrew for "groom"; in Yiddish, *chossen*

HAVDALAH   Hebrew for "separation": Saturday-evening ceremony that separates Shabbat from the rest of the week

HAVURAH   Literally, "fellowship": small, intimate participatory groups of Jews who meet for prayer, study, and celebration. Some are free-standing, some exist within synagogues. *Havurot* are generally egalitarian; they may be creative or traditional or both.

HAZZAN   Cantor

HUPPAH   Wedding canopy

KADDISH   Mourner's prayer

KALLAH   Bride (Hebrew)

KASHRUT   System of laws that govern what and how Jews eat

KETUBAH   Marriage contract

KIDDUSHIN   Sanctification: a name for the betrothal ceremony; also, a term for the entire wedding ceremony

KITTEL   White robe sometimes worn by the groom under the canopy

KLEZMER   Yiddish music and musicians

KOSHER   Permissible to be eaten according to the laws of *kashrut;* in general, proper or legitimate

MACHETUNIM   Relatives by marriage

MAVEN   An expert

MAZEL TOV   Literally, "good luck," but in practice, "Congratulations!"

MENSCH   Person; an honorable, decent person

MESADER KIDDUSHIN   One who "orders" or leads the marriage ceremony

MEZUZAH   First two paragraphs of the Shema written on a parchment scroll and encased in a small container, to be affixed to the doorposts of a home

MICHIG   Dairy foods, which, according to *kashrut*, may not be mixed with meat products

MIDRASH   Imaginative exposition of Holy Scriptures

MIKVAH   Ritual bath

MINHAG   Custom

MINYAN   Group of at least ten adult Jews (for traditional Jews, ten men; for liberal Jews, men or women) that serves as the basic unit for community prayer

MISHEGAS   Foolishness

MITZVAH   Commandment; a good deed (pl. *mitzvot)*

MIZRACHI   Jews of the Middle East and North Africa

MOTZI   Blessing over bread recited before meals

NACHES   Special joy from the achievements of one's children

NIGGUN   Wordless melody

NISSUIN   ceremony of the nuptials

ONEG SHABBAT   Literally, "Sabbath delight." In America it has become synonymous with the informal meal or snack that follows Friday-night services.

ORTHODOX   Generally, strictly traditional. The modern Orthodox movement developed in the nineteenth century in response to the Enlightenment and Reform Judaism.

PARASHA Weekly Torah portion

RABBI Teacher. "The rabbis" refers to the men who codified the Talmud.

RECONSTRUCTIONIST Religious movement, begun in the United States in the twentieth century by Mordecai Kaplan, that views Judaism as an evolving religious civilization

REFORM Movement, begun in nineteenth-century Germany, that sought to reconcile Jewish tradition and thought with modernity and the Enlightenment. Reform Judaism disputes the divine authority of Halakhah.

ROSH HODESH First day of every lunar month; the New Moon, a semiholiday

SCHMOOZ Friendly chatter

SEPHARDIM Jews from Spain, Portugal, and the Mediteranean

SHABBAT Sabbath

SHADCHAN Matchmaker

SHECHINAH God's feminine attributes

SHEHEHIYANU Prayer of thanksgiving for new blessings

SHEVA B'RACHOT Seven marriage blessings; first recited under the canopy, and following meals for seven days when a *minyan* is present

SHIDDUCH Marriage match

SHOFAR Ram's horn, blown during the High Holidays

SHTETL Small town, especially one inhabited by Ashkenazic Jews before the Holocaust

SHUL Synagogue

SIDDUR Daily and Shabbat prayerbook

SIMCHA Joy and the celebration of joy

SOFER Ritual scribe

SZATMAR Ultra-orthodox, anti-Zionist community

TAHARAT HAMISHPACHAH Laws of family purity prescribing women's sexual availability and the use of *mikvah*

TALLIS or TALLIT Prayer shawl

TALMUD Collection of rabbinic thought and laws from 200 B.C.E. to 500 C.E.

TENAIM Literally, "conditions": formal engagement contracts; also, the name of the celebration that attends the signing of the document

TORAH   First five books of the Hebrew Bible, portions of which are read every Shabbat

TSEDAKAH   Charity; righteous action toward the poor

YICHUD   "Seclusion": ten- or fifteen-minute period immediately following the marriage ceremony during which bride and groom are allowed to be alone with each other

YIDDISH   Language spoken by Ashkenazic Jews; combination of early German and Hebrew

YIDDISHKEIT   Jewishness

ZOHAR   Literally, "splendor": thirteenth-century text, the single most important book of Jewish mysticism

INDEX

ABOUT THE AUTHOR

ANITA DIAMANT was born in 1951 in Brooklyn, New York, and grew up in Newark, New Jersey, and Denver, Colorado. She holds a Bachelor's degree in Comparative Literature from Washington University and a Master's degree in English from the State University of New York at Binghamton. Upon moving to Boston in 1975, Ms. Diamant began a career in journalism. Her work has appeared in the *Boston Globe*, the *Boston Phoenix*, *Ms.*, *New England Monthly*, *Present Tense*, and *Redbook*.